Getting Skills Right

Workforce Innovation to Foster Positive Learning Environments in Canada

OECD

This work is published under the responsibility of the Secretary-General of the OECD. The opinions expressed and arguments employed herein do not necessarily reflect the official views of OECD member countries.

This document, as well as any data and map included herein, are without prejudice to the status of or sovereignty over any territory, to the delimitation of international frontiers and boundaries and to the name of any territory, city or area.

The statistical data for Israel are supplied by and under the responsibility of the relevant Israeli authorities. The use of such data by the OECD is without prejudice to the status of the Golan Heights, East Jerusalem and Israeli settlements in the West Bank under the terms of international law.

Please cite this publication as:

OECD (2020), *Workforce Innovation to Foster Positive Learning Environments in Canada*, Getting Skills Right, OECD Publishing, Paris, *https://doi.org/10.1787/a92cf94d-en*.

ISBN 978-92-64-98793-7 (print)
ISBN 978-92-64-97762-4 (pdf)

Getting Skills Right
ISSN 2520-6117 (print)
ISSN 2520-6125 (online)

Foreword

The world of work is changing. Digitalisation, globalisation, and population ageing are having a profound impact on the type and quality of jobs that are available and the skills required to perform them. The extent to which individuals, firms and economies can reap the benefits of these changes will depend critically on the readiness of adult learning systems to help people develop and maintain relevant skills over their working careers.

To explore this issue, the OECD Directorate for Employment, Labour and Social Affairs has undertaken an ambitious programme of work on the functioning, effectiveness and resilience of adult learning systems across countries. This includes the creation of the Priorities for Adult Learning (PAL) dashboard for comparing the readiness of each country's adult learning system to address future skills challenges, as well as a cross-country report, *Getting Skills Right: Future-Ready Adult Learning Systems*, which showcases relevant policy examples from OECD and emerging countries. The Directorate is also carrying out a series of in-depth country reviews of adult learning systems to offer a comprehensive analysis of the key areas where policy action is required.

This report considers how two new skills-related programmes in Canada – Future Skills and the provincial workforce innovation centers – might improve the future-readiness of Canada's adult learning system. Chapter 1 presents an overview of the Canadian labour market context and an assessment of how the adult learning system performs in international comparison. Chapter 2 examines how the new programmes might influence the future-readiness of Canada's adult learning system along five dimensions: coverage and inclusiveness; alignment of training with labour market needs; impact on labour market outcomes; finance; and governance and coordination. Chapter 3 reviews international experience in promoting high-performance work practices, and suggests how Canada's new skills-related programmes could stimulate good practice in this area.

Katharine Mullock from the Skills and Employability Division of the Directorate for Employment, Labour and Social Affairs was the main author of the report. Natasha Yokoyama, also from the Skills and Employability Division, contributed valuable research assistance. The work was carried out under the supervision of Glenda Quintini (manager of the Skills Team) and Mark Keese (Head of the Skills and Employability Division) and benefited from helpful contributions from members of the Skills team. Special thanks are due to the many Canadian stakeholders who participated in OECD meetings during the October 2019 visit to Canada, and who provided documentation and comments that were crucial inputs to the report's production. The data provided by Tahsin Mehdi (Statistics Canada) from the 2016 General Social Survey are also gratefully acknowledged.

This report is published under the responsibility of the Secretary General of the OECD, with the financial assistance of Employment and Social Development Canada. The views expressed in this report should not be taken to reflect the official position of OECD member countries.

Table of contents

FIGURES

TABLES

Follow OECD Publications on:

http://twitter.com/OECD_Pubs

http://www.facebook.com/OECDPublications

http://www.linkedin.com/groups/OECD-Publications-4645871

http://www.youtube.com/oecdilibrary

OECD Alerts http://www.oecd.org/oecddirect/

Acronyms and abbreviations

AESL	Newfoundland and Labrador Department of Advanced Education, Skill and Labour
Anact	L'Agence Nationale pour L'Amélioration des Conditions de Travail (France)
AUD	Australian dollar
AWPA	Australian Workforce and Productivity Agency
BC	British Colombia
CAD	Canadian dollar
CEGEP	*Collège d'enseignement général et professionnel*
CEI	Centre for Employment Innovation (Nova Scotia)
CHAMP	Consortium for Human Resources Development Ability Magnified Programme (Korea)
COPS	Canadian Occupational Projection System
EIF	Employer Investment Fund (United Kingdom)
EOP	Employer Ownership of Skills pilot (United Kingdom)
ESDC	Employment and Social Development Canada
EUWIN	European Workplace Innovation Network
GDP	Gross domestic product
G7	Group of Seven (Canada, France, Germany, Italy, Japan, the United Kingdom and the United States)
GIF	Growth and Innovation Fund (United Kingdom)
HPWP	High-performance work practices
HR	Human Resources
ICT	Information and communications technology
IiP	Investors in People programme (United Kingdom)
ISED	Department of Innovation, Science, and Economic Development (Canada)
LEPC	Local Employment Planning Council
LMDA	Labour Market Development Agreement
LMIC	Labour Market Information Council
NEC	National Evaluation Coordinator (United States)
NGO	Non-governmental organization
NLWIC	Newfoundland and Labrador Workforce Innovation Centre
OCWI	Ontario Centre for Workforce Innovation
OECD	Organisation for Economic Co-operation and Development
PAL	Priorities for Adult Learning dashboard
PIAAC	OECD Survey of Adult Skills
R&D	Research and development
ROI	Return on investment
SME	Small and medium-sized enterprises
SMS	Scientific Maryland Scale
Tekes	Finnish Funding Agency for Innovation, now Business Finland
TYKE, TYKES	Finland's workplace development programmes
UK	United Kingdom
UKCES	United Kingdom Commission for Employment and Skills
UKFP	United Kingdom Futures Programme
WDA	Workforce Development Agreement

WIA	Workforce Investment Act (United States)
WIC	Workforce innovation centre
WIE	Workplace Innovation Europe
WIEP	Workplace Innovation Engagement Programme (Scotland)
WIF	Workforce Innovation Fund (United States)
WIOA	Workforce Innovation and Opportunity Act (United States)
WSI	Workplace Skills Initiative (Canada)

Executive summary

By early 2020, Canada's unemployment rate had fallen to a record low level thanks to a strong economy. While this report was being finalised, however, Canada and the rest of the world were responding to a global health pandemic, COVID-19. The policy measures taken to contain the virus will have long-lasting impacts on the economy and labour markets. Early Employment Insurance claims data suggest that Canada's unemployment rate is likely to surge. While the labour market context has changed significantly, the need to learn quickly and adapt has never been greater. Initiatives like Canada's Future Skills and workforce innovation centers can help to promote new ways of working and learning.

The skills and qualifications needed in the workplace have been changing considerably as a result of digitalisation, globalisation and ageing. Middle-skilled jobs make up less of total employment than they once did, while the share of employment in high-skilled jobs has risen. Skills shortages have emerged, especially in jobs requiring a tertiary education, as well as those requiring a combination of digital, cognitive and social skills.

While Canadians are highly educated, they require opportunities to upskill and retrain throughout their working lives to remain employable as the world of work evolves. By international comparison, Canada's adult learning system performs well in two areas: alignment of training with labour market needs, and coverage (the share of adults and employers who participate in job-related training). Despite having high coverage, Canada underperforms in inclusiveness (the participation of under-represented groups in adult learning). Low-skilled and older workers – who are most at risk of job loss by new technologies – are least likely to participate in adult learning. Other areas to strengthen include flexibility, guidance, financing and the quality of training.

Canada's new skills-related programmes have the potential to improve the future-readiness of the adult learning system. The Future Skills initiative and provincial workforce innovation centres (WICs) are devoting significant public investment to testing and evaluating innovative approaches to skills development. The Future Skills Centre prioritises ways to adapt to the future labour market, while the WICs focus on improving service delivery in the current labour market. Both emphasise partnerships with labour market stakeholders. Together, these initiatives should lead to improved evidence about training programme effectiveness, which would help policy makers and practitioners select the best approaches to prepare workers for the future. By mandate, the Future Skills Centre and the WICs prioritise approaches that target under-represented groups. However, targeting low-skilled workers should be made a more explicit priority. Recommendations for how these programmes could further support a future-ready adult learning system are outlined below.

The current context invites workplaces to re-examine how they work and learn. Positioning Canada for the future requires business and government to anticipate upcoming changes, to learn quickly and to adapt. The new skills-related programmes focus on the supply side of the labour market, but the demand side is equally important. The way work is organised and people are managed matters for turning a workplace into a learning organisation. An enabling workplace environment amplifies the returns to adult learning by creating opportunities for adults to apply their newly acquired skills. Giving workers opportunities to use a broader set of skills – including creative, cognitive and social skills – also helps them to adapt to an environment where robots ably perform routine tasks. High-performance work practices – e.g. teamwork, task and working time discretion, mentoring, job rotation, incentive pay and training practices – are all strongly associated with use of a broad set of skills and informal learning. Drawing from international examples, a number of recommendations are put forward below for how Canada might stimulate good practice in this important area.

Recommendations

The following actions should be taken by Future Skills and the provincial workforce innovation centers:

Workforce innovation to support future-ready adult learning

- *Test innovative ways to engage low-skilled adults in adult learning*, including reaching out to low-skilled adults in the places they spend time. Low-skilled adults are under-represented in training despite facing a higher risk of job displacement due to automation.

- *Exploit assessments and forecasts of skill needs* in setting priorities and research agendas to help align training with labour market demand.

- *Produce and disseminate reliable information about the outcomes of training programmes.* Build the capacity of grantees to monitor the impact of their projects. Establish quality standards through the Future Skills Center to improve the impact evaluation culture in Canada, possibly following the Scientific Maryland Scale. Allocate sufficient funding to track participants' outcomes from training-related projects over the longer term. The Canadian government should also support data linkage efforts that enable researchers and policy makers to track training participant outcomes over the long-term. Disseminate evaluation evidence through webinars, in-person showcases, conferences and policy briefs.

- *Stimulate further co-financed training solutions* by requiring that successful applicants match contributions, possibly on a sliding scale so that smaller firms contribute less than larger firms do.

- *Under the leadership of the Future Skills Centre, coordinate dialogue between the WICs* through national conferences, facilitating joint projects, and building a national repository of good practice. This will promote better coordination on workforce innovation and adult learning in Canada.

Promoting skills use and learning organisations

- *Prioritise skill use and the promotion of learning organisations* in provincial workforce development strategies. Future Skills could assume a leadership role in prioritising skills use and the promotion of learning organisations as a workforce development objective.

- *Direct a portion of research funding to testing new approaches to skills use within workplaces.* Support could be targeted to testing staff and management training, the use of external experts to undertake diagnosis and upgrading of workplace organisation, or action-oriented business research. Engage social partners to build support among employers and workers.

- *Raise awareness of the benefits of effective skills use.* WICs and the Future Skills Centre should build a repository of best practices in workforce development, including firm experiences with high-performance work practices. Local actors (e.g. Ontario's Local Employment Planning Councils, workforce planning boards, and equivalent actors in other provinces) should educate employers on the benefits of HPWP and better skills use. The Canadian government should develop national HR management standards that would serve as a benchmark for firms to aspire to in creating effective learning organisations.

- *Track progress* by initiating a regular national employer survey that monitors work organisation, job design, management and training practices, as well as skills gaps.

1 Skills of the Canadian workforce

This chapter provides an overview of the labour market context in Canada, and discusses challenges related to changing demand for skills as a result of globalisation, technological change and population ageing. It provides an overview of Canada's system of adult learning.

Introduction

Canada's economy has seen robust employment growth in recent years. Linked to this growth, the job vacancy rate has hit record highs and the unemployment rate has hit record lows. Furthermore, the demand for skills is changing as a result of technological progress and globalisation. Population ageing is also putting significant pressure on the labour supply and several groups are under-represented in the labour market.

While Canada's adult population is highly educated, skills requirements are changing as the nature of work evolves. Adult learning can help adults to adapt to the changing demand for skills so that they continue to remain employable over their working lives. Investing in employees' skills is smart business for firms, as it helps to address growing skills shortages and reduce employee turnover.

This chapter describes the labour market context in Canada and the key challenges the country faces in responding to changing demand for skills. It provides an overview of the current skills of the adult population in Canada, and how the adult learning system performs in comparison to other OECD countries.

Labour market context

Tight labour market conditions in Canada

Canada's economic growth has supported strong employment growth in recent years, with the employment rate well above the OECD average and just below the level in the United States (Figure 1.1, Panel A). Fuelled by growth, the unemployment rate reached a near-record low of 5.7% in 2019 (Figure 1.1, Panel B).

Figure 1.1. Unemployment rate, Canada, United States, OECD, 2000-2019

Annual employment and unemployment rates, 2000-19

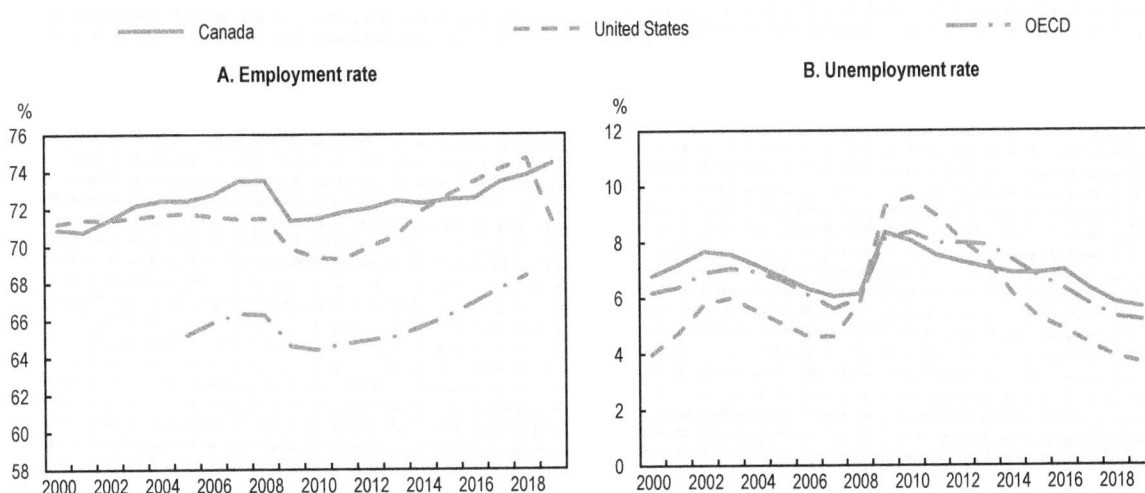

Note: Employment rate as percentage of population aged 15-64, seasonally adjusted; harmonised unemployment rate.
Source: OECD labour force statistics, https://stats-1.oecd.org/index.aspx?DatasetCode=STLABOUR.

Several additional indicators suggest tightening labour market conditions in Canada in recent years. There were 3.6 unemployed persons per vacant position (the unemployment-to-vacancy ratio) in 2016, while that ratio was down to 2.2 in 2018. Strong demand for workers is also evident from the share of firms who report labour shortages that restrict their ability to meet demand. At 31%, this share is above the historical average (Figure 1.2). The Manpower Talent Shortage Survey also tracks a rise in the share of Canadian employers reporting hiring difficulties, from 31% of employers to 41% between 2008 and 2018 (Manpower, 2018[1]), though this remains below the global average (45%). Employers in the Manpower Talent Survey cited three top reasons for their hiring difficulties: not enough applicants (26%), applicants lack experience (19%), and applicants lack required hard skills (17%). In a more general survey conducted by the Labour Market Information Council asking employers about their top HR challenges, the most common response was difficulty retaining employees (39% of employers reported this challenge). Finding qualified or skilled workers came in second (35%), followed by offering competitive wages (32%).

Figure 1.2. Labour shortages, Canada, 2008 Q1 – 2019 Q4

Share of firms that report facing labour shortages that restrict their ability to meet demand

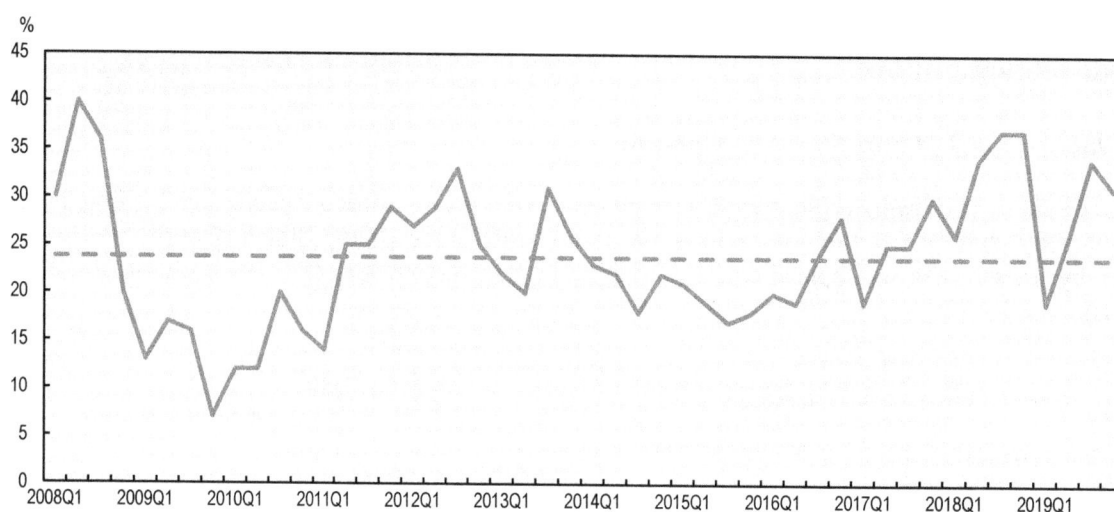

Note: The dotted line represents the historical average since 2008Q1.
Source: Bank of Canada (2020[2]), *Business Outlook Survey Winter 2019-20*, https://www.bankofcanada.ca/2020/01/business-outlook-survey-winter-2019-20/.

Some segments of the labour force are under-represented in the labour market, particularly those with a low level of education (high school or less) and persons with disabilities (Figure 1.3). Immigrants and Indigenous persons also have below-average participation rates and high unemployment rates. Removing barriers to labour force participation for under-represented groups is not only important from a well-being perspective, but also to ensure that employers have a sufficient pool of candidates to hire from in the current context of tight labour market conditions.

There is also significant variation in unemployment rates across regional labour markets (Figure 1.4): Newfoundland and Labrador (11.9%), Prince Edward Island (8.8%), and New Brunswick (8.0%) had the highest unemployment rates in 2019, while British Columbia (4.7%), Quebec (5.1%) and Manitoba (5.3%) had the lowest. In Canada's energy-intensive provinces (Alberta, Saskatchewan) unemployment rates have not yet recovered fully from the fall in oil prices in 2014.

Figure 1.3. Labour force participation and unemployment rate, selected groups, Canada, 2019*

Labour force participation rate (left axis)   ◇ Unemployment rate (right axis)

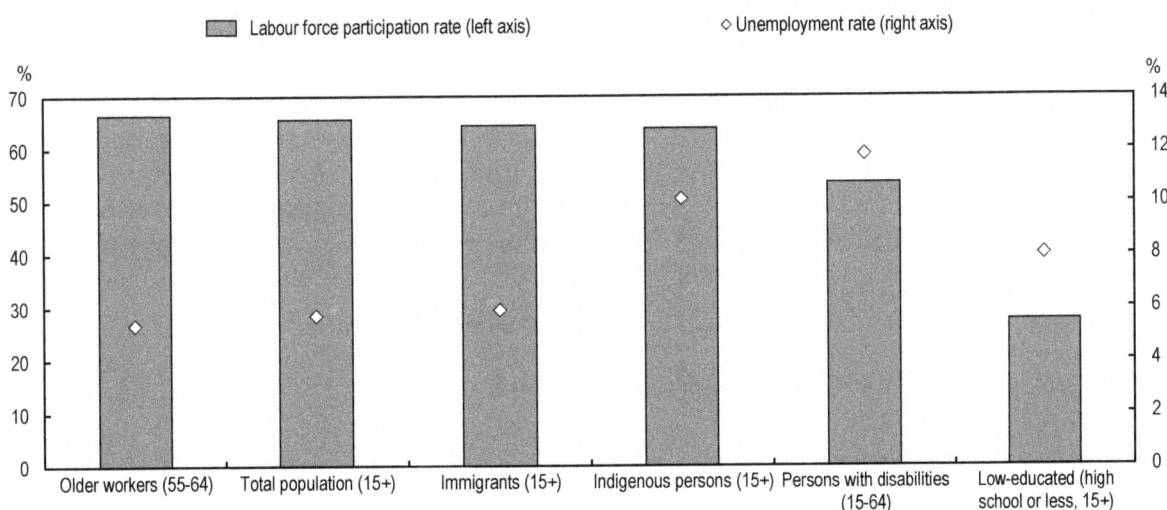

Note: * Data on persons with disabilities is from 2012. Labour force participation rate of older workers is from 2018.
Source: Statistics Canada (https://wwwstatcan.gc.ca): Table 14-10-0359-01 (Indigenous persons), Table 13-10-0348-01 (Persons with disabilities), Table 14-10-0020-01 (total population and by education level), Table 14-10-0089-01 (immigrants). OECD (https://doi.org/10.1787/8a801325-en) for labour force participation rate of older workers.

Figure 1.4. Unemployment rate, Canada and provinces, 2014 and 2019

2014   2019

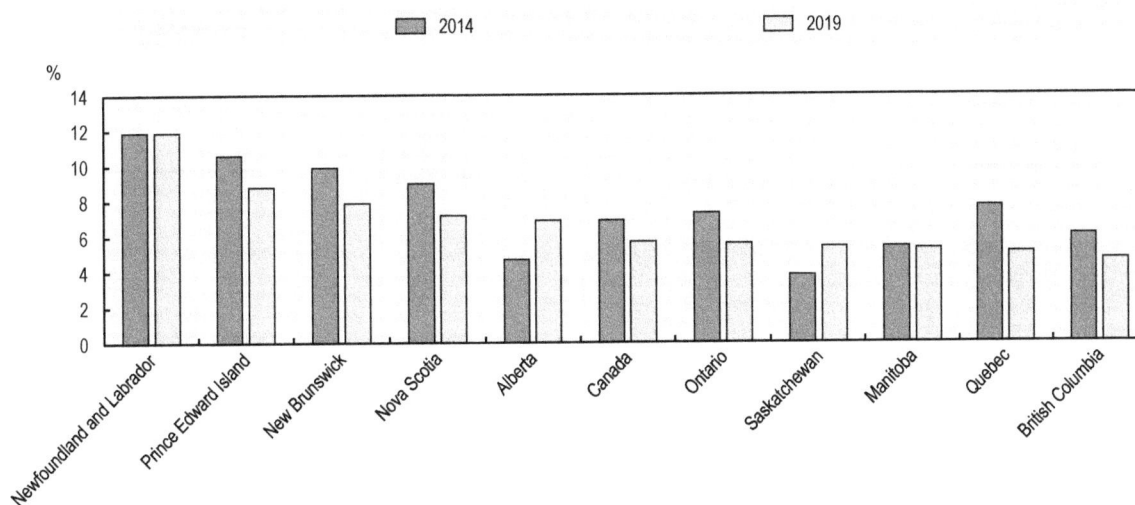

Note: Population aged 15+. Data does not include the territories.
Source: Statistics Canada. Table 14-10-0020-01, https://www150.statcan.gc.ca/t1/tbl1/en/tv.action?pid=1410002001.

Skills needs are changing

On top of tight labour market conditions due to economic growth, global trends such as globalisation, technological progress and population ageing are changing the types of skills that are in demand. These trends may lead to changes in the task content or even the destruction of some jobs, but also to the creation of new jobs that require different skills. Recent OECD research suggests that 29% of jobs in Canada are likely to see significant change in task content if current cutting-edge technology becomes widespread, and an additional 14% could be completely automated in the next 15-20 years (OECD, 2019[3]). Many Canadians could see their employability threatened unless they acquire new skills.

In terms of skill level, the new jobs are very different from those that are disappearing. Over the last two decades, OECD countries on average have seen a decline in the share of employment in middle-skilled jobs, while the share of employment in low-skilled and high-skilled jobs has risen (Figure 1.5)[1]. The phenomenon of polarisation is often explained by skill-biased technological change and a rise in demand for services. Looking at the period 1995-2015, Canada experienced a similar degree of polarisation as the United States. However, the decline in oil prices in 2014 resulted in lower demand for low-skilled workers related to the resource sector. Over 1998-2018, Canada actually saw a slight decline in the share of employment in low-skilled jobs (Figure 1.5). The decline in the share of employment in middle-skilled jobs over this period (4.1%) was entirely offset by a rise in the share of employment in high-skilled jobs (4.4%).

Figure 1.5. Job polarisation, Canada, OECD average and selected countries

Percentage point change in share of total employment, 1998 to 2018

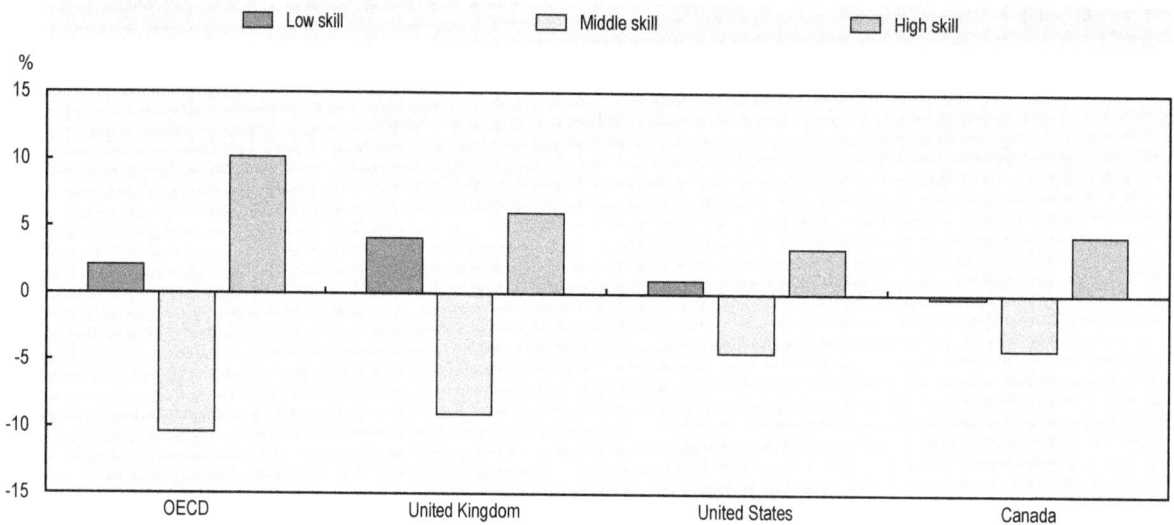

Note: High-skill occupations include jobs classified under the ISCO-88 major groups 1, 2, and 3. That is, legislators, senior officials, and managers (group 1), professionals (group 2), and technicians and associate professionals (group 3). Middle-skill occupations include jobs classified under the ISCO-88 major groups 4, 7, and 8. That is, clerks (group 4), craft and related trades workers (group 7), and plant and machine operators and assemblers (group 8). Low-skill occupations include jobs classified under major groups 5 and 9. That is, service workers and shop and market sales workers (group 5), and elementary occupations (group 9). Skilled agricultural and fisheries workers were excluded from this analysis.
Source: Updated from OECD (2017[4]), *OECD Employment Outlook 2017*, https://dx.doi.org/10.1787/empl_outlook-2017-en.

Population ageing is having an impact on both the supply of and demand for labour in Canada. Statistics Canada projects that the ratio of working-age Canadians (aged 15 to 64) to every senior (aged 65 and over) will fall from 3.9 in 2018 to 2.4 by 2055 (Department of Finance, 2018[5]). While this ratio is currently on par with the OECD average, the projected decrease over the next 20 years is one of the largest among OECD countries. An ageing population is expected to lead to a reduction in the overall labour force participation rate. This is due both to a decline in the number of working-age Canadians, and to lower labour market participation rates among older workers relative to younger workers. On the demand side, population ageing is likely to reallocate labour and other resources across sectors and occupations as demand shifts away from durable goods and towards services (such as health care).

These trends have contributed to demand for high educational qualifications. Eight of the top ten occupations in shortage in 2018, according to the OECD Skills for Jobs database, either require a post-secondary education or are management occupations (Table 1.1)[2]. According to projections carried out by Employment and Social Development Canada (ESDC) for the 2019-2028 period (Canadian Occupational Projection System), 36 out of 293 occupations analysed are expected to face labour shortage conditions and nearly all of them required a post-secondary education, apprenticeship training or were management occupations. Some 36% of occupations projected to be in shortage required a college education, compared to 53% a university degree. Only 8 of 293 occupations showed signs of surplus. Most occupations in surplus, according to both ESDC's projections and the OECD Skills for Jobs, had low qualification requirements (i.e. required no more than a secondary education or on-the-job training).

Table 1.1. Occupations in shortage and surplus, Canada, 2016-18

Occupations in shortage	Occupations in surplus
Mechanical engineers	Data entry clerks & Desktop publishing operators and related occupations
Computer engineers (except software engineers and designers)	Library, correspondence and other clerks
Mathematicians, statisticians and actuaries	Couriers, messengers and door-to-door distributors
Information systems analysts and consultants	Technical occupations in libraries, public archives, museums and art galleries
Database analysts and data administrators	Glaziers & Insulators
Software engineers and designers	Fishing vessel masters and fishermen/women
Computer programmers and interactive media developers	Other workers in fishing and trapping and hunting occupations
Mechanical engineering technologists and technicians	Labourers in textile processing & Other labourers in processing, manufacturing and utilities
Nursing co-ordinators and supervisors	
Registered nurses and registered psychiatric nurses	
Specialist physicians	
General practitioners and family physicians	
Optometrists, chiropractors and other health diagnosing and treating professionals	
Physiotherapists	
Medical laboratory technologists & Medical laboratory technicians and pathologists' assistants	
Respiratory therapists, clinical perfusionists and cardiopulmonary technologists; Medical radiation technologists & Medical sonographers	
Cardiology technologists and electrophysiological diagnostic technologists, n.e.c. & Other medical technologists and technicians (except dental health)	
Licensed practical nurses	
Nurse aides, orderlies and patient service associates & Other assisting occupations in support of health services	
Graphic designers and illustrators	
Interior designers and interior decorators	
Welders and related Machine operators	
Construction millwrights and industrial mechanics	
Heavy-duty equipment mechanics	
Industrial butchers and meat cutters, poultry preparers and related workers	

Note: National Occupational Classification (NOC) by 4-digit group.
Source: Canadian Occupational Projection System, Assessment of Recent Labour Market Conditions 2016-2018, http://occupations.esdc.gc.ca/sppc-cops/content.jsp?cid=occupationdatasearch&lang=en.

Global trends also have an impact on the types of skills in demand. The OECD Skills for Jobs database provides an international comparison of skills shortages and surpluses (Figure 1.6). In Canada, shortages are currently observed in cognitive skills including verbal, quantitative and reasoning abilities, but also in certain manual skills, such as fine manipulative abilities, endurance, and physical strength. By contrast, manual skills like these are in surplus across most OECD countries. Shortages for these manual skills in Canada are linked to relatively high shortage pressure in health care and certain technical occupations in natural resources, agriculture and related production which use these skills intensively. Canada's natural resource sector continues to be large despite the fall in oil prices, and represented 11.3% of total GDP in the first quarter of 2019.

To integrate with global markets and to thrive in the digital workplace, workers need not only strong digital and cognitive skills, but also social and emotional skills, such as management, communication, and self-organisation skills (OECD, 2017[6]; OECD, 2019[7]). Social skills – including coordination, instructing, negotiating, persuasion, service orientation and social perceptiveness – are found to be in shortage in Canada according to the Skills for Jobs database. This is consistent with a domestic analysis of online job postings. It found that employers looking for digital skills are generally also looking for a candidate with strong "soft" skills, including communications and organisational skills, interpersonal skills, and writing skills (Vu, Lamb and Willoughby, 2019[8]). Similarly, the top three skill groups employers were looking for in a separate study of online job vacancies were business management, leadership and oral communication – all social and emotional skills (LMIC, 2019[9]).

Figure 1.6. Skills in shortage and surplus, Canada and OECD average, 2018

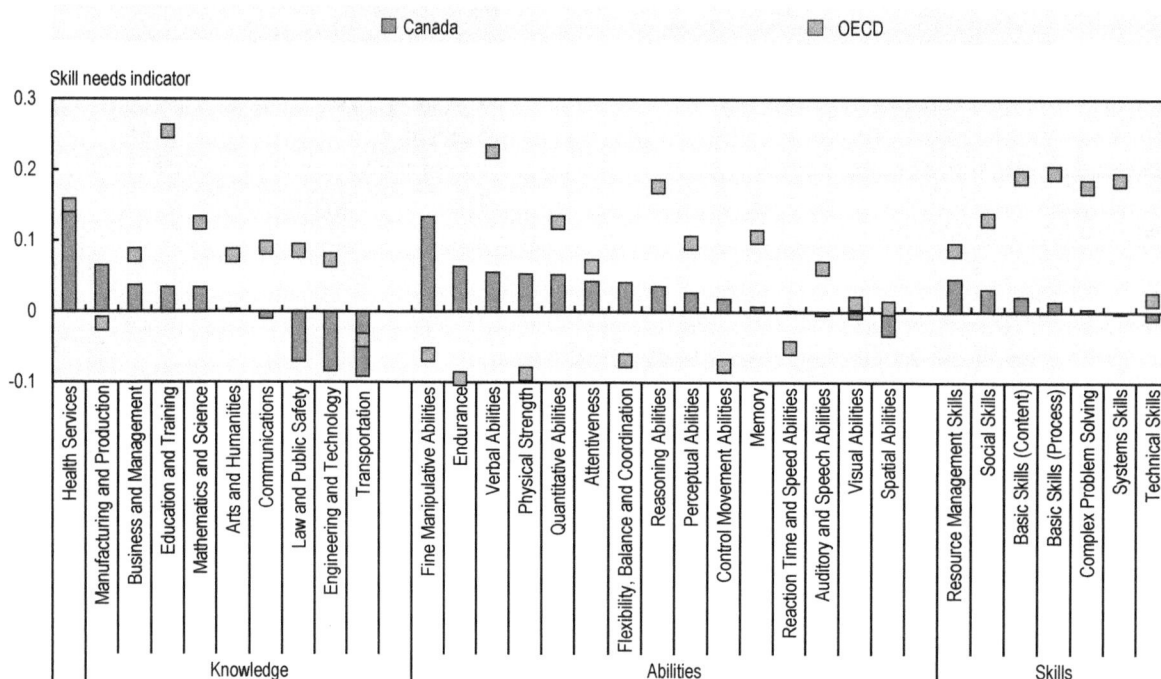

Note: Positive values indicate shortages while negative values indicate surpluses. The indicator is rescaled to have a maximum value of one across skill types and OECD countries. The indicator is a composite of five sub-indices: wage growth, employment growth, growth in hours worked, unemployment rate and growth in under-qualification. Data on unemployment by previous occupation are not available for Canada, and hence the indicator is based on only four sub-indices. The OECD average refers to the latest available year.
Source: OECD Skills for Jobs database, www.oecdskillsforjobsdatabase.org.

Skills of the adult population

Most adults have a tertiary education, but many have low literacy or numeracy skills

Canada has the highest share of tertiary-educated workers across the OECD: 58% of Canadian adults aged 25-64 had a tertiary education in 2018, compared with the United States at 47%, and the OECD average at 37%. These figures result from the large number of students graduating from college programmes in Canada (26% of adults in 2018, compared with 11% in the United States and 7% across the OECD)[3]. Canada performs closer to the OECD average in university-level educational attainment (a bachelor's degree or higher) (Figure 1.7).

Figure 1.7. Adults with a university education, OECD countries, 2018

Share of adults aged 25-64 with a university education

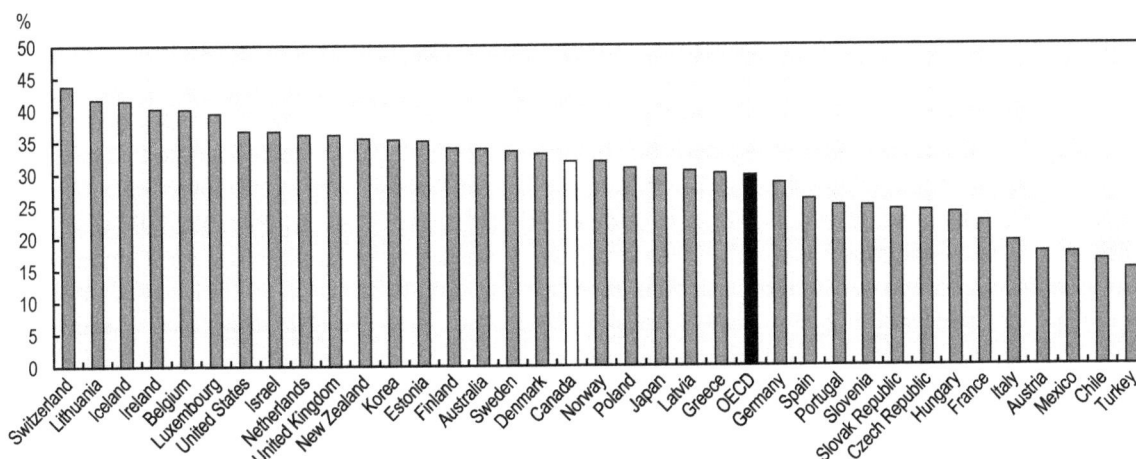

Note: Data for Chile is for 2017.
Source: OECD (2019[10]), *Education at a Glance 2019: OECD Indicators*, https://dx.doi.org/10.1787/f8d7880d-en.

Canada is above average, but below top performers, in the skills assessed by the OECD Survey of Adult Skills: literacy, numeracy and problem solving in technology-rich environments. A sizeable share of Canada's adults – 27% – have low performance in either literacy or numeracy, scoring at Level 0 or 1 (Figure 1.8). Canada's large foreign-born population (22% of the population were not born in Canada) may help to explain why this share is so high. While foreign-born adults in Canada are highly educated, quite often their first language is neither English nor French. They tend to have lower proficiency in the language of survey assessment (English or French) relative to Canadian-born adults. Indeed, 39% of foreign-born Canadians score at Level 0 or 1 in literacy or numeracy compared to only 21% for the native-born population. This disadvantage also makes it harder for foreign-born adults to integrate into the Canadian labour market.

Figure 1.8. Adults with low literacy or numeracy skills, OECD countries, 2012/15

Share of adults aged 25-64 scoring at proficiency Level 0 or 1 in literacy or numeracy

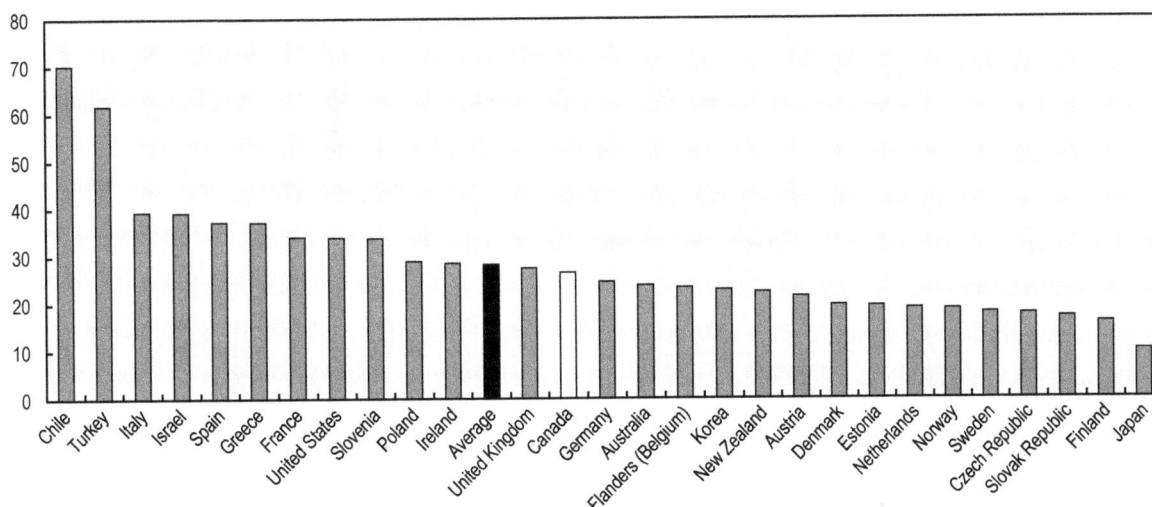

Source: OECD Survey of Adult Skills (PIAAC, 2012, 2015). Twenty-four countries, including Canada, participated in the first round of the Survey of Adult Skills in 2012. Nine countries took part in the second round in 2015.

Mismatch by qualifications, field of study, and skills

While most university graduates work in jobs that require a university education, a portion do not. One measure of over-qualification is the share of graduates who are not working in occupations usually requiring their highest level of educational attainment. In Canada, 16% of individuals (15-64) were over-qualified for their job in 2016, on par with the OECD average (OECD Skills for Jobs database). A similar share of adult workers (18%) self-reported being over-qualified in the 2016 General Social Survey. Immigration plays a role in explaining over-qualification in Canada. University-educated immigrants – especially those who did not graduate in Canada or the United States – are significantly more likely than Canadian-born graduates to report being over-qualified (Uppal and Larochelle-Côté, 2014[11]). Lower English and French language skills, difficulties assessing foreign credentials and lack of Canadian work experience are part of the explanation, but discrimination may also be a factor. A Statistics Canada study (Larochelle-Côté and Hango, 2016[12]) shows that over-qualified university graduates tend to employ their literacy, numeracy and digital problem-solving skills less in the workplace than their well-matched counterparts.

Field of study mismatch occurs when workers who were educated in a particular field work in a different one. According to the 2016 General Social Survey, about 36% percent of Canadian adults are working in a field different from the one in which they studied (very close to the 37% reported by adults in the 2012 Survey of Adult Skills). Field of study mismatch is the result of both labour supply and demand factors. These include the degree of saturation of a particular field in the labour market and the level of transferable skills offered by a particular field of study. While field of study mismatch is lower in Canada relative to the average (39%) (Montt, 2015[13]), it may be costlier: 42% of adults who are mismatched by field of study are also overqualified for their jobs (above the average of 33%) (Montt, 2015[13]). Field of study mismatch generally only leads to costs for economies when combined with over qualification.

Figure 1.9. Over-skilling rate, Canada, 2016

Percentage of adults who report having the skills to cope with more demanding duties in their job

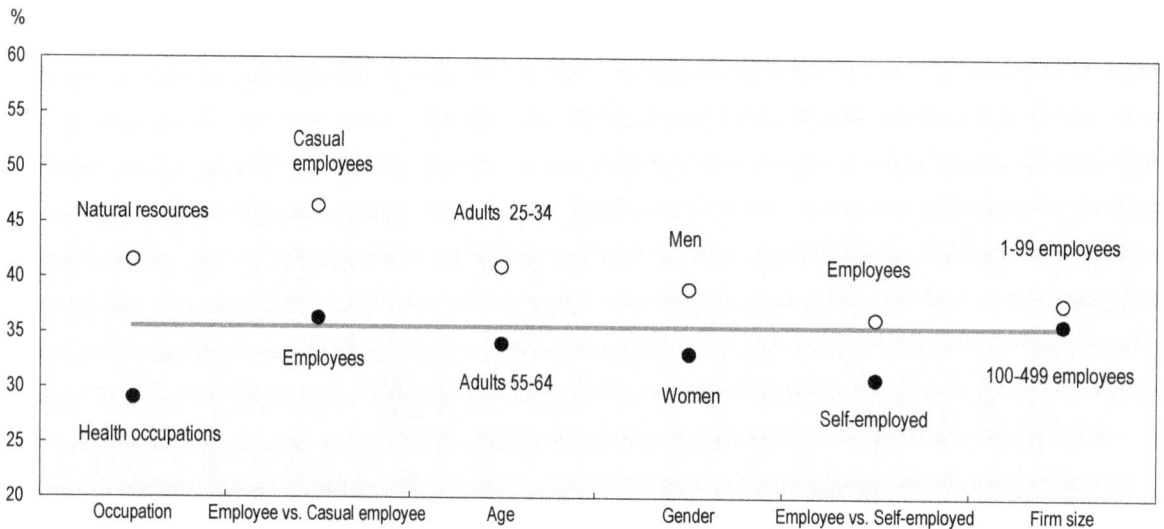

Note: Population of employed adults aged 25-64. This chart shows the groups with the highest and lowest rates of over-skilling by category. The rates of over-skilling by education, immigration status and union status are not shown. There was very little variation between these groups. Casual employees also includes on-call employees.
Source: 2016 General Social Survey. Author's calculations using the public-use micro-data file.

Some 43% of Canadian adults report a poor match between their job and skills. A large share (35.5%) of Canadian adults report that they have the skills to cope with more demanding duties in their job, i.e. they are over-skilled (Figure 1.9). Only 7.5% report that they are under-skilled and require training to cope with their current duties. The incidence of over-skilling is higher among certain groups: men, younger adults aged 25-34, and casual or on-call employees. As adults age and become better matched to their roles, the rate of over-skilling declines. Being self-employed is also associated with lower rates of over-skilling. The rate of over-skilling does not vary significantly by education, union status or immigration status. The highest rates of over-skilling are in natural resources, agriculture and other production occupations, as well as sales and service occupations. Individuals working in health occupations display the lowest rate of over-skilling.

Adult learning policy context and performance

How well individuals, firms and economies adapt to the changing world of work described above critically depends on the readiness of a country's adult learning system to help people develop and maintain relevant skills over their working careers. This section provides an overview of Canada's adult learning system.

Box 1.1. Defining adult learning

This report focuses on the population of potential adult learners aged 25-64. Adults in this age group have generally completed initial education and have begun their working lives. Adult learning can be classified as formal education, non-formal education or informal learning.

Formal education: institutionalised learning activities (e.g. seminars, courses, on-the-job training, open and distance education) which are a minimum of one semester and which are recognised as programmes by the relevant education or equivalent authorities.

Non-formal education: institutionalised learning activities which are either of short duration (less than one semester of full-time equivalent) or are not recognised by the relevant education or equivalent authorities.

Informal learning: non-institutionalised learning activities that are unstructured (e.g. no student/teacher interaction) and can take place anywhere, e.g. learning while doing.

Source: Eurostat (2016[14]), *Classification of Learning Activities Manual*, https://dx.doi.org/10.2785/874604.

Overview of Canada's adult learning system

Education in Canada is primarily a provincial and territorial responsibility, and there is no single pan-Canadian approach to adult learning. Provincial and territorial ministries responsible for education plan and implement policies for adult learning and skills development with financial support from the federal government, and often in consultation with other government sectors, non-governmental organisations, or the private sector. The federal government also plays a strong role in skills development to support Canada's labour market competitiveness

While provision of adult learning varies by jurisdiction, Table 1.2 provides an overview of the general types of programmes available in Canada and the institutions that offer them. Programmes include literacy and essential skills programmes for adults, English or French as a second or additional language, vocational education and training, apprenticeships, higher education, adult liberal education (i.e. hobby courses) and workplace training. Programmes are delivered by a wide range of agencies, organisations and institutions including school boards, colleges, cégeps[4], vocational centres, universities, adult learning centres, Indigenous owned-and-operated post-secondary institutions, community groups, non-profit and volunteer groups, employers, unions, associations, private companies, and special groups serving specific types of learners (e.g. Indigenous learners, immigrants, women, prisoners, low-income and unemployed individuals).

Table 1.2. Structure of adult learning provision in Canada

	Adult basic and general education	Adult vocational education	Adult higher education	Adult liberal education	Workplace training
Programmes	English or French as a second language Literacy and essential skills General Equivalency Diploma High school diploma University preparation	Diploma Apprenticeship	Bachelor's degree Master's degree Doctoral degree Professional certification	Non-formal learning	Courses commissioned by employers
Institutions	Adult education centers Community groups Non-profit and volunteer groups Associations	Colleges Technical institutes Cégeps Vocational centers	Universities	Universities Colleges Adult education centers Community groups Non-profit and volunteer groups Associations	Firms Universities Colleges Private providers Adult education centers

Note: The list of institutions providing adult learning programmes depicted in this chart is not comprehensive.
Source: Elaborated by the author based on the framework from Desjardins (2017[15]), *Political Economy of Adult Learning Systems*, https://dx.doi.org/10.1007/s11159-017-9670-1.

Many universities and colleges have special admission processes for mature students (adults who have been out of school for at least one year). Universities and colleges often make allowances for mature students to carry out part or all of their degree or diploma requirements on a part-time or evening basis, by distance or online. In 2017/18, there were 691 000 adults (age 25+) enrolled in post-secondary programmes. The most common post-secondary programmes that adults enrolled in were degrees (45% of adult post-secondary learners), followed by diplomas (17%), followed by certificates (13%)[5].

Unemployed individuals access employment and training services by registering with the provincial public employment service. One of the programmes available to registered jobseekers is skill development. The objective of the skill development programme is to assist active and former Employment Insurance claimants in obtaining the skills they need for employment (ESDC, 2017[16]). Funded programmes include essential skills training, adult basic education, English or French as a second language, and occupational skills training. New federal legislation enables unemployed adults to continue receiving employment insurance benefits while pursuing full-time training.

There are no pan-Canadian budget indicators of overall spending on adult learning. But the federal government invests close to CAD 7.5 billion annually in skills development for Canadians, and CAD 3 billion of this is delivered in partnership with the provinces and territories (Department of Finance, 2019[17]). These transfers fall under two major bilateral agreements: the Workforce Development Agreements[6] (WDA) and the Labour Market Development Agreements (LMDA). WDAs support skills upgrading, work experience programmes, and assistance setting up a new business. LMDAs support programmes to help unemployed people find work and to ensure a skilled labour force that meets the needs of employers. The design and delivery of the programmes and services funded under these agreements are the responsibility of provinces and territories. They do not need to be approved by the federal government.

The federal government also invests in skills development for adults outside of its partnerships with the provinces and territories. This includes direct support to learners through targeted training programmes for Indigenous persons, persons with disabilities, and recent immigrants. It also includes student financial assistance. In the 2018/19 fiscal year, the federal government invested over CAD 3.5 billion in loans and CAD 1.6 billion in non-repayable grants. Student financial assistance is available to all students, regardless of age.

The 2019 budget report announced a new financial incentive to promote adult learning participation. The Canada Training Benefit fills a gap identified by the 2018 Horizontal Skills Review which found that unemployed Canadians receive a broad range of supports to acquire or develop new skills but that working adults in mid-career could benefit from more support (Department of Finance, 2019[17]). The Canada Training Benefit includes a refundable tax credit up to CAD 5 000 to offset tuition costs and related fees, as well as an Employment Insurance Training Support Benefit to compensate income lost while training. It also includes leave provisions for federally regulated workers to take time away from work for training while maintaining their job security.

Canada's performance on adult learning

The OECD Priorities for Adult Learning (PAL) dashboard facilitates cross-country comparisons on the future-readiness of adult learning systems (Figure 1.10).

Figure 1.10. Priorities for Adult Learning dashboard, Canada and the OECD average

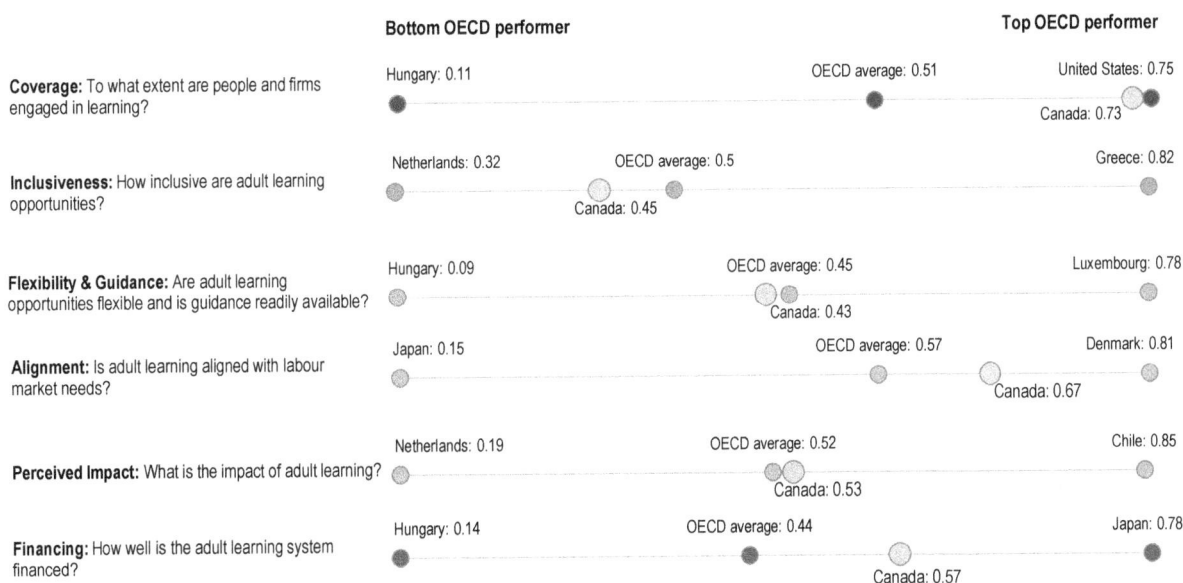

Source: Priorities for Adult Learning dashboard, http://www.oecd.org/employment/skills-and-work/adult-learning/dashboard.htm.

Canada performs above the OECD average in two areas: alignment of training with labour market needs and coverage. Aligning training with labour market needs depends on high quality labour market information. Canada invests in an array of initiatives to generate information about labour and skills needs. The Labour Market Information Council was established in 2017 to improve the timeliness, reliability and accessibility of labour market information. Canada also performs well on coverage, i.e. the share of Canadian adults and employers who participate in job-related training. Just over half (52%) of the working-age population participated in at least one job-related training activity within the previous 12 months, according to the 2012 OECD Survey of Adult Skills (Figure 1.11). This compares with an OECD average of only 41% of adults. According to the 2016 General Social Survey, two-thirds (66%) of adult Canadians received some type of training (not limited to job-related training) in 2016.

Despite having high coverage in adult learning compared to other countries, Canada performs relatively poorly in inclusiveness. In particular, participation rates are low among low-skilled workers, low-waged workers, older workers, the unemployed, those working in small and medium-sized enterprises (SMEs) and those in temporary work[7].

Figure 1.11. Adult participation in formal or non-formal job-related training OECD, 2012

Share of adults aged 25-64 who participated in job-related training

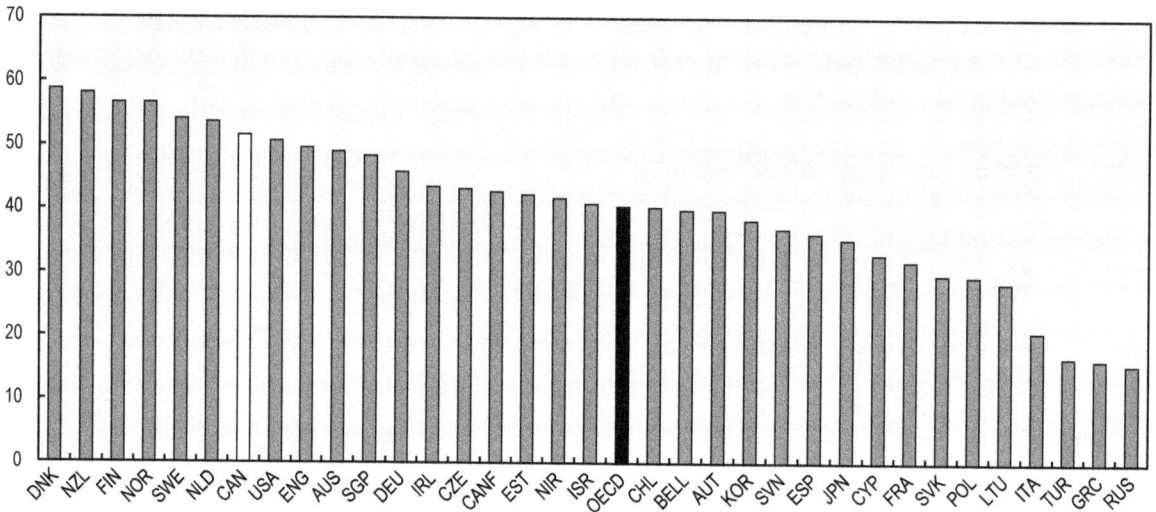

Note: Job-related training includes all forms of skill development that participants identify as being motivated by reasons related to current or future employment. Job-related learning can occur either in the classroom or in the workplace, and it can be sponsored by an employer, government or by the individual learner.
Source: OECD Survey of Adult Skills (PIAAC, 2012, 2015).

Notably, Canada displays one of the largest gaps in participation rates between high/medium-skilled workers and low-skilled workers (Figure 1.12). Across OECD countries, low-skilled workers participate much less than higher-skilled workers in training, but this gap is particularly large in Canada (28 percentage points relative to 23 percentage points). While changes in skills requirements due to technological change affect all workers, the growing demand for high-level cognitive skills and complex social interaction skills suggest that low-skilled workers in jobs that are intensive in repetitive or manual tasks are likely to bear the brunt of these changes (OECD, 2019[3]). Despite having a greater need for upskilling, low-skilled workers receive less training than high-skilled workers.

The participation gap between the prime-age population (25-54) and older adults (55+) is also larger in Canada relative to the average (23 percentage points vs. 21 percentage points). Unless older workers upgrade the skills they acquired in initial education, many are likely to experience skills obsolescence due to technological change. Given the shorter period of time that older workers have to recoup the investment in training before retirement, they tend to receive less training than younger workers. Workforce innovation programmes are testing ways to bridge these gaps and will be discussed in Chapter 2.

Figure 1.12. Inclusiveness of adult learning opportunities, Canada and OECD, 2012
Percentage point differences in training participation rates between groups

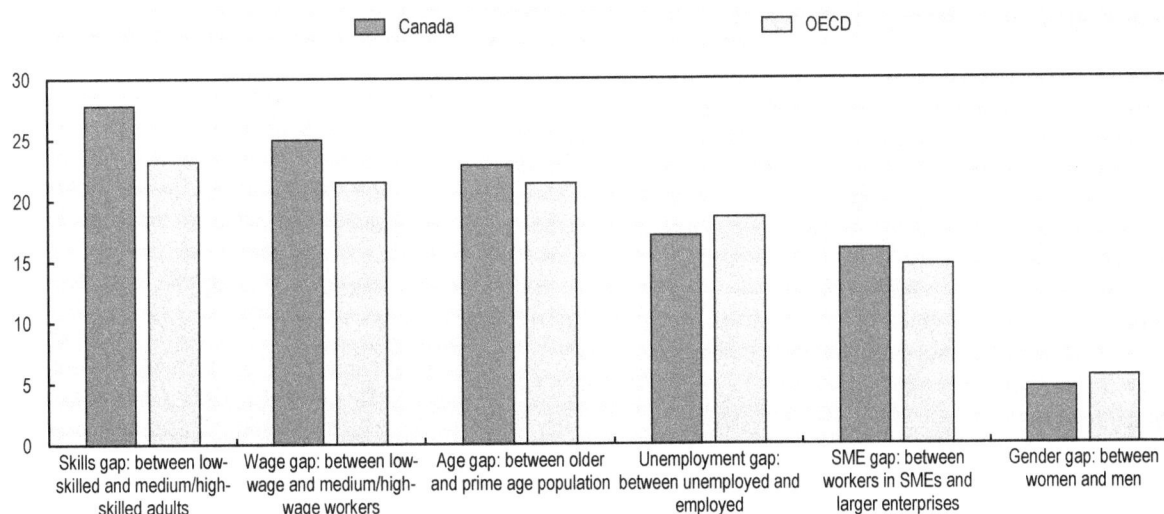

Note: Participation in formal and non-formal job-related education and training.
Source: OECD Survey of Adult Skills (PIAAC, 2012, 2015)

On other dimensions, including flexibility and guidance, Canada performs in the middle of the pack. Do adults have access to guidance about learning opportunities? Are learning opportunities available in flexible formats, including online, distance, modular, part-time or evenings? Flexible modes of training delivery can make training more accessible for adults who struggle to find time to train. Being too busy at work was the main barrier cited by Canadian adults who wanted to train more (30%) (Figure 1.13). Another 17% reported that they did not have time due to childcare and family responsibilities. Some 12% said the course was not offered at a convenient time or place. There are signs that Canadians are making use of flexible modes of training delivery. Some 10% of the population aged 16-65 participated in open or distance education in 2012, on par with the OECD average. The Conference Board of Canada also tracked a shift away from formal classroom training towards informal learning, as an increasing number of employees initiate their own self-paced e-learning (The Conference Board of Canada, 2018[18]).

Figure 1.13. Main reason for not training, Canada and the OECD average, 2012

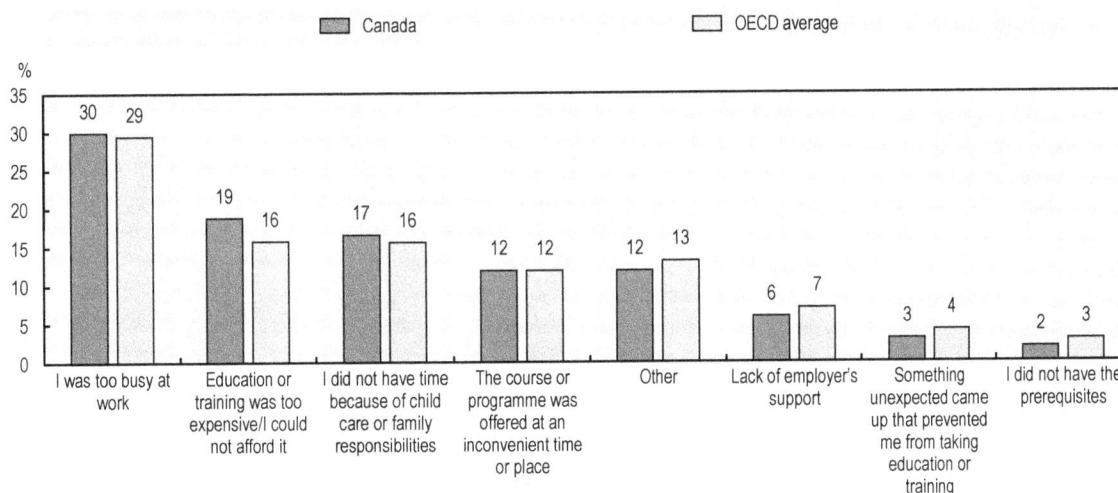

Note: Adults who wanted to participate more in formal or non-formal job-related training over the last 12 months but were unable to do so.
Source: OECD Survey of Adult Skills (PIAAC, 2012, 2015).

Another area where Canada performs close to average is in financing. In Canada, the personal financial cost of training represents the second most important barrier to participation (Figure 1.13). Some 19% of adults in Canada who wanted to participate more in training did not do so because it was too expensive, which is above the OECD average (16%).

The third area where Canada's dashboard performance only ranks as average is on the impact of training. To assess whether training has a positive impact on labour market outcomes, the PAL dashboard considers various indicators: wage returns, self-reported usefulness of training, and whether adults have opportunities to use newly acquired skills in the workplace. Wage returns to training in Canada are higher than the OECD average (10% versus 8.5%), though adults in several countries enjoy greater returns to training (Chile, Lithuania, Estonia, Poland, Ireland, United Kingdom). Some 62% of adult learning participants report that at least one training activity was "very useful" for their job (PIAAC). On this measure, Canada outperforms the average (52%), and yet falls behind Denmark (82%) and New Zealand (66%). More recent data from the 2016 General Social Survey suggest stronger performance: 87% of Canadian adults who participated in training in the last 12 months reported that it helped improve job performance. However, a lower share reported that it helped to improve future job prospects (68%). An even lower share said that it improved job security (55%).

To translate newly acquired skills into higher productivity, job satisfaction and wages, adults need opportunities to deploy their skills in the workplace (OECD, 2016[19]). As noted above, the 2016 General Social Survey suggests that 35.5% of Canadian adults have the skills to cope with more demanding duties in their job. The OECD Survey of Adult Skills asks how often workers use reading, writing, numeracy, information and communication technology (ICT) and problem solving skills at work. Canada generally performs above the OECD average on the use of each type of skill (Figure 1.14). However, both the United States and Australia surpass Canada, suggesting potential to improve. Having opportunities to deploy their skills at work has an impact on employee job satisfaction and as a result, employee engagement. According to Gallup's Employee Engagement survey with data collected from 2014 to 2016[8], only 20% of Canadian workers reported feeling engaged at work (Gallup, 2017[20]). This percentage is higher than the global average (15%) but much lower than the United States (33%).

Figure 1.14. Average use of information-processing skills at work, OECD countries

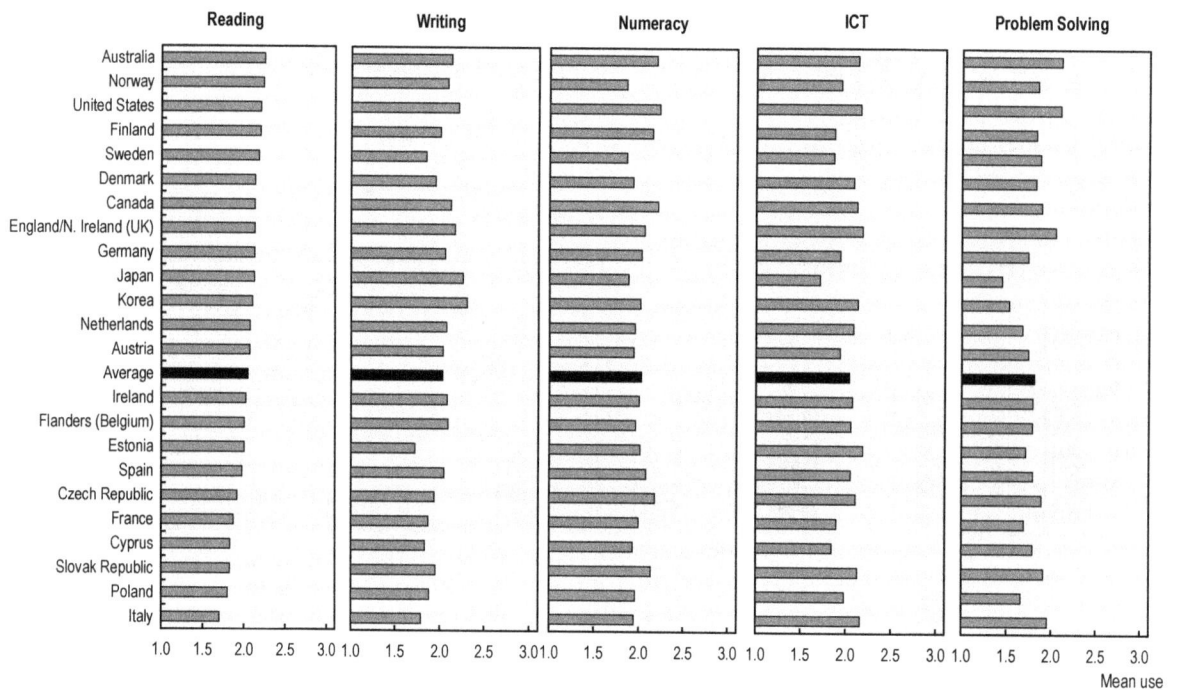

Source: OECD Survey of Adult Skills (PIAAC, 2012, 2015).

Prioritising better skills use benefits in several ways. It not only improves the impact of adult learning, but it also advances the national productivity and innovation agenda (Stone, 2011[21]). Labour productivity growth in Canada lags behind the United States and other G7 countries (Figure 1.15). It has done so since the 1980s (Rao, Tang and Wang, 2008[22]). Analysts offer various explanations for Canada's puzzling lower productivity, including an insufficient innovation culture, low capital intensity growth, and poorer infrastructure. The United States' productivity advantage may also arise from the way that American workplaces provide employees with opportunities to use their skills. A skilled workforce does not guarantee actual skills usage. In fact, skills proficiency explains only a small fraction of the variation (OECD, 2019[23]). Dedicated efforts are needed to understand and improve skills use in the Canadian workplace. Policy responses to improve skills use in the workplace will be discussed in Chapter 3.

Figure 1.15. Labour productivity growth, Canada, United States, G7 and OECD, 2003-2018

Annual percentage change in GDP per hour worked

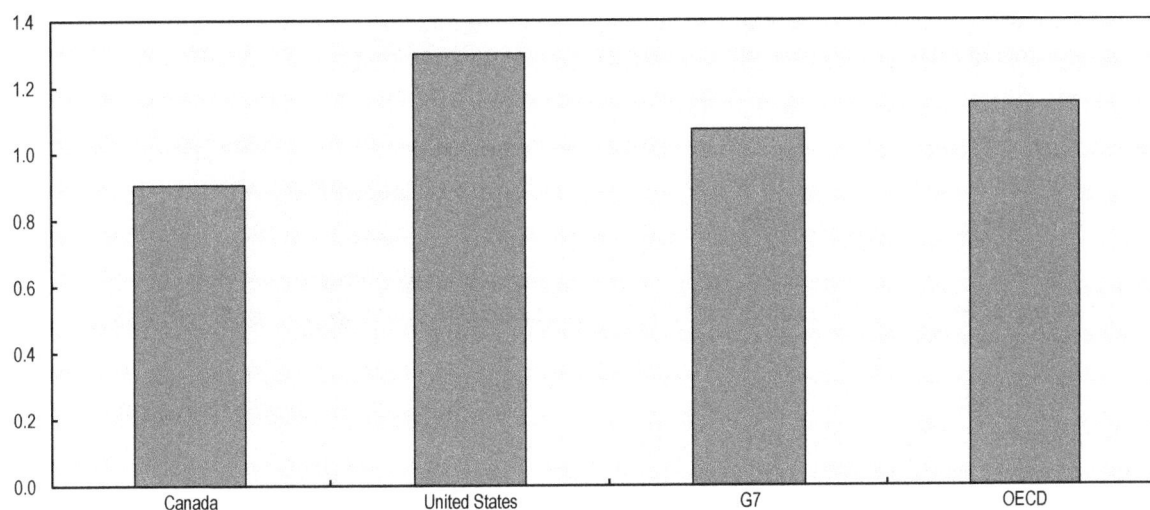

Source: OECD (2019[24]), OECD Compendium of Productivity Indicators 2019, https://dx.doi.org/10.1787/b2774f97-en.

Summary

The skills and qualifications needed in the workplace have been changing considerably as a result of digitalisation, globalisation and population ageing. Middle-skilled jobs make up less of total employment than they once did, while the share of employment in high-skilled jobs has risen. Skills shortages have emerged, especially in jobs requiring a tertiary education, as well as those requiring a combination of digital, cognitive and social skills.

Canada needs to take a critical look at its current adult learning system. Is it well equipped to deal with the pressing challenges associated with changing demand for skills? Workers whose skills have become obsolete with technological change could benefit from retraining in higher-demand skill areas. In addition to supporting transitions from one occupation to another, Canada's adult learning system should equip adults with the foundational skills needed to weather evolving changes in skills demand, including social skills, verbal, reasoning and quantitative abilities. A sizeable share of the adult population has low English or French literacy skills, and the share is particularly high among the immigrant population. Upgrading these skills could improve the labour market integration of immigrants. In doing so it would address skills shortages by making better use of the skills of immigrants, who are highly educated.

Canada's adult learning system performs well in international comparison, particularly on coverage and alignment of training with labour market needs. A key challenge will be how to engage workers who typically enjoy lower access to adult learning opportunities, including older and low-skilled workers, . A sharper focus on flexibility, guidance, financing and the impact of training will support these goals.

There have been interesting recent developments in workforce innovation in Canada. The next chapter assesses their potential to improve the future-readiness of adult learning systems with reference to the dimensions above.

References

Bank of Canada (2020), "Business Outlook Survey Winter 2019-20", Bank of Canada, https://www.bankofcanada.ca/2020/01/business-outlook-survey-winter-2019-20/. [2]

Department of Finance (2019), "Budget 2019: Investing in the Middle Class", Canadian Department of Finance, Ottawa, https://www.budget.gc.ca/2019/docs/plan/budget-2019-en.pdf. [17]

Department of Finance (2018), "Update of Long-Term Economic and Fiscal Projections", Department of Finance, Government of Canada, https://www.fin.gc.ca/pub/ltefp-peblt/2018/report-rapport-eng.asp. [5]

Desjardins, R. (2017), "Political economy of adult learning systems: Comparative study of strategies, policies and constraints", *International Review of Education*, Vol. 64/2, pp. 265-267, http://dx.doi.org/10.1007/s11159-017-9670-1. [15]

ESDC (2017), *Evaluation of the Labour Market Development Agreements: Synthesis Report*, Employment and Social Development Canada, Ottawa, https://www.canada.ca/en/employment-social-development/corporate/reports/evaluations/labour-market-development-agreements.html. [16]

Eurostat (2016), "Classification of learning activities (CLA) manual: 2016 edition", European Union, Luxembourg, http://dx.doi.org/10.2785/874604. [14]

Gallup (2017), "State of the Global Workplace", Gallup Press, http://file:///C:/Users/Mullock_K/Downloads/State%20of%20the%20Global%20Workplace_Gallup%20Report%20(1).pdf. [20]

Larochelle-Côté, S. and D. Hango (2016), "Overqualification, skills and job satisfaction", in *Insights on Canadian Society*, Statistics Canada, Ottawa, https://www150.statcan.gc.ca/n1/en/pub/75-006-x/2016001/article/14655-eng.pdf?st=sALLE4ge (accessed on 16 December 2019). [12]

LMIC (2019), *Insights into skills and jobs advertised on LinkedIn in 2018*, Labour Market Information Council, https://lmic-cimt.ca/wp-content/uploads/2019/03/LMIC_LinkedIn-LMI-Insights-No-10.pdf (accessed on 26 September 2019). [9]

Manpower (2018), *Solving the Talent Shortage: Build, Buy, Borrow and Bridge*, Manpower Talent Shortage Survey, https://manpowergroup.ca/campaigns/manpowergroup/talent-shortage/pdf/canada-english-talent-shortage-report.pdf (accessed on 16 December 2019). [1]

Montt, G. (2015), "The causes and consequences of field-of-study mismatch: An analysis using PIAAC", *OECD Social, Employment and Migration Working Papers*, No. 167, OECD Publishing, Paris, https://dx.doi.org/10.1787/5jrxm4dhv9r2-en. [13]

OECD (2019), *Education at a Glance 2019: OECD Indicators*, OECD Publishing, Paris, https://dx.doi.org/10.1787/f8d7880d-en. [10]

OECD (2019), *OECD Compendium of Productivity Indicators 2019*, OECD Publishing, Paris, https://dx.doi.org/10.1787/b2774f97-en. [24]

OECD (2019), *OECD Employment Outlook 2019: The Future of Work*, OECD Publishing, Paris, https://dx.doi.org/10.1787/9ee00155-en. [3]

OECD (2019), *OECD Skills Outlook 2019 : Thriving in a Digital World*, OECD Publishing, Paris, https://dx.doi.org/10.1787/df80bc12-en. [7]

OECD (2019), *OECD Skills Strategy 2019: Skills to Shape a Better Future*, OECD Publishing, Paris, https://dx.doi.org/10.1787/9789264313835-en. [23]

OECD (2017), *OECD Employment Outlook 2017*, OECD Publishing, Paris, https://dx.doi.org/10.1787/empl_outlook-2017-en. [4]

OECD (2017), *OECD Skills Outlook 2017: Skills and Global Value Chains*, OECD Publishing, Paris, https://dx.doi.org/10.1787/9789264273351-en. [6]

OECD (2016), *OECD Employment Outlook 2016*, OECD Publishing, Paris, https://doi.org/10.1787/empl_outlook-2016-en. [19]

Rao, S., J. Tang and W. Wang (2008), "What Explains the Canada-US Labour Productivity Gap? on JSTOR", *Canadian Public Policy*, Vol. 34/2, pp. 163-192, https://www.jstor.org/stable/25463606. [22]

Skolnik, M. (2018), "Factors Contributing to Canada's Number One International Ranking in the Proportion of Adults Who Have Attained a Community College Credential", Centre for the Study of Canadian and International Higher Education, http://www.oise.utoronto.ca/cihe (accessed on 27 January 2020). [25]

Stone, I. (2011), "International approaches to high performance working. Project Report.", UK Commission for Employment and Skills, London, http://www.ukces.org.uk/publications/er37-international-approaches. [21]

The Conference Board of Canada (2018), *Canadian Employers' Investment in Employee Learning and Development Continues to Rise*, https://www.conferenceboard.ca/press/newsrelease/2018/01/31/canadian-employers-investment-in-employee-learning-and-development-continues-to-rise?AspxAutoDetectCookieSupport=1. [18]

Uppal, S. and S. Larochelle-Côté (2014), "Overqualification among recent university graduates in Canada", http://www.statcan.gc.ca, (accessed on 25 November 2019). [11]

Vu, V., C. Lamb and R. Willoughby (2019), "I, Human: The digital and soft skills driving Canada's labour market", https://brookfieldinstitute.ca/report/i-human-the-digital-and-soft-skills-driving-canadas-labour-market/. [8]

Notes

[1] Estimates of labour market polarisation are sensitive to the methodology used to define low-, middle-, and high-skilled occupations. The skill level of occupations can be approximated in different ways, including by educational requirements, complexity of tasks, and wages. The OECD methodology divides occupations into skill categories based on their ISCO-88 major group. High-skill occupations include jobs classified under the ISCO-88 major groups 1, 2, and 3. That is, legislators, senior officials, and managers (group 1), professionals (group 2), and technicians and associate professionals (group 3). Middle-skill occupations include jobs classified under the ISCO-88 major groups 4, 7, and 8. That is, clerks (group 4), craft and related trades workers (group 7), and plant and machine operators and assemblers (group 8). Low-skill occupations include jobs classified under major groups 5 and 9. That is, service workers and shop and market sales workers (group 5), and elementary occupations (group 9). Skilled agricultural and fisheries workers were excluded from this analysis.

[2] The remaining two occupations in shortage are sales-related occupations, which have low educational and skill requirements. These occupations are considered to be facing shortage pressure due to their above-average growth in wages and hours worked in recent years.

[3] Skolnik (2018[25]) observes that Canada's high rate of attainment of short-cycle tertiary education is due to its emphasis on the role of non-university post-secondary institutions – colleges and institutes – in the provision of programmes of two or three years' duration.

[4] A cégep (Collège d'enseignement général et professionnel) is a publicly-funded post-secondary education pre-university technical college exclusive to the province of Quebec.

[5] Statistics Canada, Table: 37-10-0015-01, Postsecondary enrolments, by credential type, age group, registration status, programme type and gender.

[6] The Workforce Development Agreements consolidate the former Canada Job Fund Agreements and the Labour Market Agreements for Persons with Disabilities.

[7] Based on a derived variable of disability status in the 2016 General Social Survey, Canadian adults with a disability were equally likely to participate in learning opportunities as adults without a disability.

[8] Gallup's overall engagement measure is based on survey responses to questions about overall satisfaction at work, clarity of expectations, adequate materials and equipment, opportunity to do what one does best, recognition of good work, having someone at work who cares, feeling that one's opinions count, clarity about organisational mission or purpose, and having opportunities to learn and grow.

2 Workforce innovation to support future-ready adult learning

Workforce innovation involves testing, sharing and implementing new approaches to employment and training services. This chapter provides an overview of recent developments in workforce innovation in Canada. It assesses their potential to improve the future-readiness of Canada's adult learning system along five dimensions: coverage and inclusiveness, alignment of training with labour market needs, impact of adult learning, financing, and governance.

Introduction

In the last five years, Canada has introduced a number of skills-related policies and programmes that have altered the policy landscape and have the potential to improve the future-readiness of Canada's adult learning system. In February 2019, Future Skills was launched at the national level, providing a platform to identify emerging skills and workforce trends, to build partnerships, and to test and evaluate innovative approaches to skills assessment and development. Several provinces (Newfoundland and Labrador, Nova Scotia, Quebec, British Columbia, Manitoba and Ontario[1]) have established "workforce innovation centres" since 2015, with a mandate to test and share innovative models of workforce development (Box 2.1). Most of the initiatives supported by these bodies focus on the supply side of the labour market (e.g. skills development, matching jobseekers with jobs, reducing barriers for under-represented groups).

This chapter provides an overview of these new initiatives. Importantly, it seeks to assess the extent to which they could influence the future-readiness of Canada's adult learning system based on five dimensions, referred to in Chapter 1, and set out in the OECD Future-Ready Adult Learning framework (OECD, 2019[1]): coverage and inclusiveness, alignment of training with labour market needs, impact of adult learning, finance, and governance and coordination.

Box 2.1. Definition of workforce development, workforce innovation, and workplace innovation

Workforce development generally describes a labour market strategy that includes both employment and training services. It involves the coordination of public and private sector activities, policies and programmes to create and sustain a workforce that can support current and future business and industry.

Such strategies complement traditional employment services. The main difference between workforce development and traditional employment services is that while employment services focus on matching a single job seeker to a job, workforce development is focused on solutions for groups of job seekers or employed workers and often involves multiple employers (Zizys, 2018[2]).

The definition of "workforce" is broad, and includes individuals who will soon be employed (i.e. young adults), currently employed workers, job seekers including the unemployed, individuals currently out of the labour force (e.g. retirees and individuals in prisons), as well as individuals recruited from abroad.

Workforce innovation refers to the testing, sharing and implementation of new approaches to workforce development. The OECD Directorate for Science, Technology and Innovation defines innovation as "a new or improved product or process (or combination thereof) that differs significantly from the unit's previous products or processes and that has been made available to potential users (product) or brought into use by the unit (process)." In the context of workforce development, an innovation might be the use of an online tool to better match jobseekers with employers based on skills, or a programme to retrain rapidly a group of workers in declining industries. Closer collaboration (e.g. between actors from the demand and supply sides of the labour market or from across sectors) that improves service delivery might also constitute an innovation in this context.

Workplace innovation is a type of workforce innovation. It is the testing, sharing and implementation of new approaches to work organisation, management practices and job design that leads to better use of workers' skills and more learning in the workplace. Workplace innovation is discussed in Chapter 3 along with the related concepts of high-performance work practices and skills utilisation.

Source: Jacobs, R., and J. Hawley (2009[3]), "The Emergence of 'Workforce Development': Definition, Conceptual Boundaries and Implications"; http://dx.doi.org/10.1007/978-1-4020-5281-1_167T, Zizys (2018[2]) , "Workforce development, demand-led strategies and the goal of good jobs", https://ocwi-coie.ca/wp-content/uploads/2018/08/01-018-01-Zizys-Tom-Final-Report.pdf.

New programmes in workforce innovation

National level: Future Skills

The 2017 federal budget first announced Future Skills as part of Canada's Innovation and Skills Plan. Amid disruptive changes in labour markets due to technological advancements, new business models and population ageing, Future Skills is the response to calls from the Advisory Council on Economic Growth and the Forum of Labour Market Ministers for new approaches to addressing skills gaps and supporting lifelong learning. With federal government funding of CAD 225 million over 2018-22 and CAD 75 million per year thereafter, Future Skills has a mandate to foster partnership across sectors; identify emerging skills and workforce trends; test and evaluative innovative approaches to skills assessment and development; and share information to inform future investments and programming. With half of available funding dedicated to addressing the needs of underrepresented and disadvantaged groups, it places a particular emphasis on ensuring that all Canadians have a fair chance to benefit from emerging opportunities. Recognising provincial and territorial governments' responsibilities with respect to skills development, the Canadian government has involved provincial and territorial governments in the design and implementation of Future Skills through the Forum of Labour Market Ministers.

Future Skills includes the Future Skills Council and the Future Skills Centre. The Future Skills Council works collaboratively with members from the public and private sectors, labour, education and training providers, not-for-profit and Indigenous organizations to provide coherent advice to the Minister of Employment, Workforce Development and Disability Inclusion on emerging skills needs and workforce trends. The Council is developing a Strategic Plan based on consultations with a diversity of stakeholders nationwide. The plan will set out a vision for Canada to position jobseekers, workers and employers for success. It will identify priority areas for action to ensure that skills development and training programmes meet new workplace demands.

The Future Skills Centre is an independent applied research and innovation body funded through an agreement with Employment and Social Development Canada (ESDC). The Future Skills Centre prototypes, tests and evaluates innovative approaches to skills assessment and development, with a focus on how to prepare workers to succeed in the future labour market (Table 2.1). It disseminates the results of its applied research widely to encourage broader adoption of proven practice.

The Centre has the flexibility to identify projects through open calls as well as through solicited and unsolicited proposals. To date, the Centre has initiated 16 innovation projects worth CAD 19 million over two years. Some of the areas of focus include upskilling and reskilling models for mid-career workers; innovative approaches to support transitions into the digital industry sector; and supporting Indigenous peoples in skill development.

A key underlying objective is for analysis and evidence generated by the Council and Centre to inform actions taken by public, private, labour, education and training providers, and not-for-profit organizations. Through ESDC's Future Skills Office, the Government works with provincial and territorial partners as well as horizontally across the federal government to support the integration of knowledge of "what works" into policy and programme design. Doing so positions Canada to leverage innovation in order to accelerate workforce transitions.

Table 2.1. Classification of projects, the Future Skills Centre

Projects selected from the first two calls for proposals

	Number of projects
Retraining a group of workers or job seekers to transition into a high-demand occupation or sector	6
Upskilling a group of workers to remain employable or to progress in their existing jobs	7
New approaches to matching job seekers with jobs, career counselling, job search	8
Addressing non-skill related barriers to employment	3
Addressing non-skill related barriers to education and training	8
Improving labour market systems and services through research and evaluation	0
New approaches to work organisation, management practices or job design within firms	0
Total number of projects (after first two calls for proposals)	16

Note: The rows do not add up to the total because some projects can be classified in more than one way.

Box 2.2. Examples of Future Skills Centre projects

Helping older workers to overcome fear and uncertainty around retraining

The project developed by the Northern Lights College in British Columbia will specifically target mid-career workers interested in making a career change. It will engage 200 participants and provide them with support in identifying a retraining programme, selecting the right programme, and meeting admissions requirements. Project participants will benefit from an online platform ("Continuous learning for individuals' mid-career and beyond", CLIMB) to help them identify risks to their jobs posed by automation, their individual strengths, how their skills match with employers' needs, and to create a personalised skills training plan.

Retraining mid-career manufacturing and steelworkers in Alberta and Ontario

A partnership between three trade unions and an adult learning provider, this project focuses on early engagement with workers who are at risk of displacement due to automation in manufacturing. Two hundred mid-career workers will be part of this two-year programme that will include identifying workers' skills, assisting employers and unions in setting up workplace training that addresses skills gaps, and connecting workers with new employment opportunities. Workers will retrain either for new jobs within the company or outside of the company.

Source: Future Skills Centre website, https://fsc-ccf.ca/.

Provincial level: Workforce Innovation Centres

Six Canadian provinces have established workforce development agencies that share several common functions, including supporting applied research, testing new approaches to workforce development, acting as hubs and coordinating bodies for sectoral partners, and communicating generated evidence to government and stakeholders. This report will refer to these agencies collectively as "workforce innovation centres" or WICs (see Box 2.3 for a list of WICs). WICs are funded through federal-provincial Labour Market Development Agreements (LMDA).

The specific mandate of each WIC varies by province (Box 2.3). For instance, the Newfoundland and Labrador, Nova Scotia and former Ontario WICs put strong emphasis on funding community-based and practitioner-led research, while British Colombia and Quebec focus on research and capacity building of labour market stakeholders. The newly opened Manitoba WIC funds training, but without a research component (i.e. without an emphasis on evaluating and identifying best practices which might be applicable elsewhere). Coordination and information sharing between the five WICs is not formalised but takes place through regular conference calls.

The Future Skills Centre performs the same functions as the WICs, with one key distinction: it prioritises approaches that help workers to adapt to the future labour market, while the WICs focus on improving service delivery in the current labour market. The Future Skills Centre is required to engage with labour market stakeholders across the country, including WICs. Doing so improves coordination and prevents duplication of efforts.

Box 2.3. Workforce innovation centres in Canada

Newfoundland and Labrador Workforce Innovation Centre (2017-present)

The NL Workforce Innovation Centre (NLWIC) provides funding for community-based research to test models of workforce development that will influence employability, entrepreneurship and attachment to the workforce in Newfoundland and Labrador.

Centre for Employment Innovation (Nova Scotia) (2016-present)

The Centre for Employment Innovation (CEI) was awarded to St. Francis Xavier University in June 2016. The CEI supports community-based research to improve the quality of employment services in Nova Scotia.

Ontario Centre for Workforce Innovation (2016-2019)

The Ontario Centre for Workforce Innovation was established in 2016 at Ryerson University with funding from the Government of Ontario. The Ontario Centre funded innovative research and evaluation to identify and test solutions to workforce development challenges. Its purpose was to provide a single coordinated source of best practices on how to deliver evidence-based employment and training programmes in Ontario. It operated five regional hubs before shutting down in 2019.

Quebec Observatoire Compétences-emplois (2010-present)

Founded by the Government of Quebec's Commission des partenaires du marché du travail in 2010, the Quebec Observatoire Compétences-emplois (OCE) brings together researchers and stakeholders from different sectors to develop research and innovation projects on workforce development. Its mission is to support labour market stakeholders in thinking and acting innovatively to foster a skilled workforce in Quebec.

Northern Workforce Development Centre (Manitoba) (2018-present)

The Northern Workforce Development Centre was set up in 2018 at the University College of the North (UCN) Thompson campus to facilitate workforce transitions from training to employment. The Centre focuses on providing training and certification to help Northern Manitoba workers compete in the skilled labour market.

BC Centre for Employment Excellence (2012-2017)

The British Columbia Ministry of Social Development and Poverty Reduction created the BC Centre for Employment Excellence in 2012. Its mandate was to support the research and information needs of BC service providers, practitioners, and employers involved in the employment services sector. Funding through the LMDA ended in 2017, but the Centre continues to be managed as a sub-division of the Social Research and Development Corporation.

The Newfoundland and Labrador Workforce and Innovation Centre (NLWIC) was chosen as a case study for this report. NLWIC's stated goal is "to support the research, testing and sharing of ideas and models of innovation in workforce development." The ultimate aim is to have a positive impact on employability, employment and entrepreneurship in the province's labour force, and particularly among under-represented groups. Funding comes through the Newfoundland and Labrador Department of Advanced Education, Skills and Labour (AESL) under the Canada-Newfoundland and Labrador LMDA. College of the North Atlantic acts as an operating partner, assisting with calls for proposals, project accountability, communications, capacity building and stakeholder engagement.

Since its inception in 2017, the NLWIC has had two calls for proposals, with 20 projects receiving CAD 7.66 million in total funding (Table 2.2). Projects range in duration from a year and a half to three years, with CAD 383 000 per project on average. Projects are selected based on whether they promote workforce and skill development in growth sectors (tourism, oil and gas, fisheries, forestry, and healthcare services) as identified by the province's strategic vision document. Eight of the projects have a skills development component. Projects without a skills development component focus on overcoming non-skill related barriers to employment or education and training (e.g. mental health, transportation, or cultural barriers) or improving approaches to matching jobseekers with jobs.

The value-added of the NLWIC, according to stakeholders, is that it creates a network of community-based research that did not exist before. It is an opportunity for practitioners to influence policy making.

While the WICs receive funding through federal-provincial LMDAs, they are also eligible to apply for funding from the Future Skills Centre. To date the only example of this is a partnership between the Future Skills Centre and the Nova Scotia Centre for Employment Excellence. They are collaborating to test a virtual reality technology to train professional drivers in the trucking industry. The industry is at risk of disruption from the automation of vehicles. There is scope for further partnership between WICs and the Future Skills Centre. For example, WICs could apply for funding to test the replicability of successful approaches in different parts of the country.

Table 2.2. Classification of Projects, Newfoundland and Labrador Workforce Innovation Centre

Projects selected from the first two calls for proposals

	Number of projects
Retraining a group of workers or job seekers to transition into a high-demand occupation or sector	2
Upskilling a group of workers to remain employable or advance in their existing jobs	6
New approaches to matching job seekers with jobs, career counselling, job search	6
Addressing non-skill related barriers to employment	9
Addressing non-skill related barriers to education and training	4
Improving labour market systems and services through research and evaluation	3
New approaches to work organisation, management practices and job design within firms	0
Total number of projects (after first two calls for proposals)	20

Note: The rows do not add up to the total because some projects can be classified in more than one way.

Box 2.4. Examples of NLWIC funded projects

Retraining in the tourism sector

Hospitality Newfoundland and Labrador and Tourism Canada partnered to identify and deliver training for employed and unemployed workers from non-tourism industries to support the expansion of rural tourism destinations. Five regions with high tourism potential and high unemployment or low workforce participation were prioritised. After assessing the baseline skills of participants, each participant will be directed to either broad-based classroom retraining or more targeted training depending on their needs.

Preparing refugees for work in the agriculture sector

In light of provincial shortages in skilled farm labour as well as low participation of refugees in the labour market, this project aims to connect skilled refugee farmers to agricultural employment. The project is led by the Association for New Canadians in partnership with Memorial University. Refugee farmers received training in English farming terminology, safety, and knowledge about local industry. Of the 15 participants who received training, 11 were offered interviews, eight were offered jobs, and five accepted. One of the key challenges is that agricultural opportunities are far from urban centres where refugee families typically settle.

Online delivery of literacy training to low-skilled workers in rural areas

Newfoundland and Labrador has the highest share of adults without a high school diploma in Canada (15.7% of working-age adults compared to the national average of 11.5%). One of the challenges of upskilling these adults is that 60% of the province's population lives in a rural area and many lack the computer and literacy skills needed to access online education and training. The project will develop an online learning platform to deliver literacy training in a way that mimics the platforms learners already use (e.g. Facebook, Twitter). The project is led by Newfoundland and Labrador Laubach Literacy Council Inc.

Source: NLWIC website (http://www.nlwic.ca/research-support-projects/funded-projects/) as well as project updates provided by participants.

Local level

Many actors at the local and sectoral levels across Canada are involved in testing, implementing and sharing innovative practices to workforce development. Chambers of Commerce, industry boards on colleges, and workforce planning boards, among others, play a role in coordinating the demand side and supply side responses to ensure that the workforce is evolving to meet the needs of the changing economy.

Two local efforts that we encountered in Ontario are worth highlighting. Ontario's network of Local Employment Planning Councils (LEPC) is a pilot programme to promote place-based approaches to workforce development (Box 2.5). LEPCs collect local data to identify the workforce development needs of employers in their region. They help to align the actions of stakeholders in the community to respond better to workforce development challenges. Another example of local workforce innovation is Palette, a Toronto-based talent platform. In June 2019, Palette launched its first programme, SalesCamp, specifically targeting workers from disrupted industries looking to transition into new careers in the knowledge sector. Collaborating with employers in the technology industry, Palette built a 6-week training programme in tech sales; 95% of programme graduates received a job offer within 8 months (Box 2.6).

Box 2.5. Ontario's Local Employment Planning Councils

Eight Local Employment Planning Councils (LEPC) were established in Ontario in 2015 as a pilot programme "to promote place-based approaches to workforce development, while generating and analysing local labour market information" (Government of Ontario, 2018[4]). Seven of the eight LEPC contracts were awarded to former workforce planning boards. An evaluation carried out two years after the start of the pilot concluded that the LEPCs have become a central hub for employment, training and workforce issues in their communities. They have also been successful in developing and maintaining collaborative relationships with a diverse range of community partners.

Engaging employers, particularly SMEs, is challenging due to the limited time and capacity employers have to step away from business. Successful approaches have included meeting with employers in their place of business, allowing flexibility in the nature and duration of employers' contributions, targeting employers by sector, shortening employer survey tools, and sharing tailored and concise information at events and through social media posts. The Peterborough LEPC runs a speaker series and the Peel-Halton LEPC offers webinars, both educating employers on workplace issues such as inclusive hiring practices, mental health, gender and diversity, and workplace safety. Several LEPCs offer online tools, such as platforms to match employers with job seekers, and "HR toolkits" to support recruitment, hiring and retention of a skilled workforce.

LEPCs collect and analyse local labour market information to identify the workforce development priorities and needs in their communities. For instance, the Peel-Halton LEPC analyses data from employer and employee surveys to help Milton employers better understand their difficulties hiring general labourers. Transportation was determined to be a key barrier, since public transit in this area is minimal, and high housing costs in Milton mean that workers must commute long distances. Milton residents tend to be highly educated, while the difficult-to-fill general labourer positions are low-skilled positions. The LEPC is using their analysis to engage employers in finding collective solutions, including mobilising employers to contribute to the cost of renting a van to bring workers to Milton.

The Peel-Halton LEPC conducts research to understand the impact of automation on local industries. It has identified a mismatch in the skills required by growing industries in high tech and those available among workers from traditional industries. Their next step is to identify training and employment pathways for current and future industry workers who may be displaced by automation. The Peterborough LEPC undertakes research and outreach activities to educate employers about the benefits of "experiential learning" (defined as opportunities to work in a workplace or on a work project), particularly for high-demand industries in their region (healthcare, manufacturing, agriculture and tourism). The Peterborough LEPC sees itself as a "one stop shop" for employers to learn about employment and training services, including literacy and digital skills training offered by local providers.

Initial LEPC funding ran from December 2015 to May 2017, but currently runs until 2020 after being renewed three times. A key challenge identified by LEPCs in planning longer-term activities was the short funding cycles and the short notice given regarding funding extensions. The evaluation recommended extending the funding agreements for a full planning cycle (3-5 years) to allow enough time to observe longer-term impacts and to enter into longer-term employment contracts with staff. At the time of this report's publication, LEPCs had received word that the pilot would end in April 2020 and LEPCs would return to operating as workforce planning boards.

Source: OECD interviews with representatives from the Ottawa, Peel-Halton and Peterborough LEPCs.

Box 2.6. Palette: an upskilling and retraining pilot

Palette is a talent platform based on the hypothesis that there are workers in declining industries with the foundational skills needed by growing industries. Supported by the federal Sectoral Initiatives Program, Palette launched "SalesCamp" in June 2019. Sales Camp is a 6-week training programme (one week intensive in-person training, three weeks of blended learning and online group work) designed to prepare workers from declining industries (e.g. retail, food and hospitality and customer support) for jobs in growing industries, such as business-to-business sales for tech firms. The programme targets workers who have held customer-facing roles and already have the necessary foundational skills to work in tech sales, but need upskilling specific to the tech industry. Palette stresses a demand-driven model where employers contribute to the development of the curriculum in collaboration with a selected training institution. Palette brings employers directly into the classroom to witness and take part in live sales assignments, case studies, panels and networking events. Some 37 participants and 19 tech companies participated in the first two cohorts, with 95% of graduates receiving job offers within eight months of programme completion. A new boot camp launched in March 2020 focuses exclusively on placing female participants in tech sales. Palette has received an additional CAD 5 million over three years from FedDev Ontario to implement similar upskilling programmes in Durham and Windsor regions.

Source: Palette, https://paletteskills.org/.

Canada's model in international comparison

Table 2.3 provides an overview of the workforce innovation programmes in Canada, the United Kingdom, Australia and the United States. No other OECD country shares exactly the same model as Canada. However, the models in United Kingdom, Australia and the United States share similarities. The What Works Network in the United Kingdom consists of 13 independent What Works Centres, including a regional affiliate centre in Wales. The What Works Centres test and evaluate approaches to skills development, as does the Future Skills Centre, but they also address other areas of policy (e.g. policing, local economic growth, and health and social care). Australia's Try, Test and Learn Fund performs similar functions to Canada's Future Skills Centre, though it does not have the same degree of independence since it is run by the Department of Social Services. One state in Australia (Victoria) has a workforce training innovation fund similar to Canada's provincial workforce innovation centers. There are no apparent ties between the federal fund and the fund in Victoria. There are clear ties in the United States between the federal Workforce Innovation Fund and the state workforce development boards. Boards compete for grants under the fund, as in Canada where WICs and LEPCs may collaborate with the Future Skills Centre and lead on research projects. In Canada, the Future Skills Centre is required to engage with the workforce innovation centers and other labour market stakeholders to ensure efforts are not duplicated and to learn from one another.

The subsequent section assesses the potential of Canada's new programmes to improve the future-readiness of Canada's adult learning system, drawing lessons from the experiences of other countries, but particularly the United Kingdom, Australia and the United States.

Table 2.3. Workforce innovation programmes in Canada, United Kingdom, Australia and the United States

	Canada	United Kingdom	Australia	United States
National	Future Skills	What Works Network	Try, Test and Learn	Workforce Innovation Fund
Sub-national	Workforce innovation centres		Victoria Workforce Training Innovation Fund	State Workforce Development Board

Potential of new initiatives to improve Canada's adult learning system

This section adopts the framework outlined in OECD (2019[1]) and referenced in Chapter 1 to assess the potential of Future Skills, the WICs, and Ontario's LEPCs to make Canada's adult learning system more future ready along the following dimensions:

- **Coverage and inclusiveness**: Broad-based coverage in adult learning is necessary to support a rewarding and inclusive future of work.

- **Alignment of adult learning provision with labour market needs**: For adult learning to improve a participant's labour market prospects, adults must train to develop skills that employers need, and those needs are constantly changing.

- **Impact of adult learning**: To have the desired impact on labour market outcomes, reliable information about the quality and outcomes of training programmes is needed, as are actual opportunities to apply the newly acquired skills in the workplace.

- **Financing**: Ideally, adult learning systems receive adequate financing through a mix of co-financing provided by employers, individuals and governments.

- **Governance and co-ordination**: With so many actors involved in adult learning, strong coordination mechanisms are essential to ensure coherent policy.

Coverage and inclusiveness

Broad-based coverage in adult learning is necessary to support a rewarding and inclusive future of work. Just over half (52%) of adults participate in adult learning in Canada. This is higher than the OECD average but lower than top-performing countries like Denmark (59%) and New Zealand (58%). Moreover, individuals most at risk of displacement due to automation are often under-represented in adult learning (see Chapter 1). Offering information and guidance, removing barriers to participation, targeting support, and engaging employers are strategies used across countries to improve participation.

The underlying premise behind Future Skills and the WICs is that by building the evidence base around what works and what does not work in adult skills development, programme effectiveness will improve and more people will benefit. Many of the projects funded under the Future Skills Centre and NLWIC aim to improve coverage and inclusiveness in access by removing barriers for under-represented groups. Both the Future Skills Centre and WICs specifically target projects that address skills challenges faced by under-represented groups in the labour market. Often these people are also under-represented in adult learning participation. The Future Skills Centre is required to dedicate half of its funding to addressing the needs of under-represented and disadvantaged groups. For instance, the most recent call for proposals from the Future Skills Centre targeted retraining solutions for mid-career workers. Older workers are likely to experience significant skills obsolescence in the context of technological change unless they upgrade the skills they acquired in initial education. However, employers are often reluctant to invest in the skills of older workers, given shorter periods to recoup this investment before retirement. One of the selected Future Skills Centre projects attempts to address barriers faced by older workers by developing an online platform. Using the platform, workers self-assess their skills and create a personalised skills training plan (Box 2.2). Another under-represented group targeted by Future Skills and the WICs is Indigenous persons. A project funded by the NLWIC involves a college collaborating with Indigenous partners to make the college admissions process more accessible for mature (aged 19+) Indigenous students.

More efforts seem to be needed to actively reach out to low-skilled adults in the places they spend time – workplaces, community institutions and public spaces. One of the reasons underlying low representation of low-skilled adults in adult learning, in Canada and elsewhere, is that adults with low skill levels find it more difficult to recognise their learning needs. They hence are less likely to seek out training opportunities

(Windisch, 2015[5]). The Future Skills Center and WICs could support creative solutions and partnerships that would more actively engage low-skilled adults in training. International approaches for engaging low-skilled workers in training could be tested and adapted to the Canadian context. For instance, the Viennese project *Mama lernt Deutsch! – Mum is learning German!* provides basic skills training for mothers with a low level of education and for whom German is not their first language. The programme takes place in their child's educational institution and includes free child-care services. In Belgium, the Brussels-based project *Formtruck* is a mobile walk-in information centre about learning opportunities. It reaches out to low-qualified jobseekers and young people not in employment, education or training in locations where they usually spend time, e.g. at events, parks and public squares. Additional examples of international approaches for engaging low-skilled workers in training can be found in OECD (2019[6]).

The Future Skills Centre and WICs also support greater coverage in adult learning by testing innovative modes of training delivery. Flexible provision of adult education and training addresses the most commonly reported barrier, that of limited time. Many countries offer learning provision on a part-time basis, in the evenings, on weekends, as distance learning, or in a modular and/or credit-based format. Projects supported through the Future Skills Centre and WICs can test and provide evidence about the effectiveness of flexible modes of training delivery. For instance, the "career pathways" model tested by the Ontario Centre for Workforce Innovation is a compelling approach to retraining adult learners. It combines modular learning with career guidance (Box 2.7). In Newfoundland, an NLWIC project developed an online tool to raise literacy and digital skills among adults in rural communities, in order to facilitate their access to online education and training.

A focus on the coordination of employment and training services can support greater participation in adult learning. Ontario's LEPCs facilitate employers' access to existing employment and training services, including Employment Ontario providers, Ontario Works, Ontario Disability Supports Program, and Literacy and Basic Skills. Through Employer Help Desks and Talent Hubs, employers can reach out to LEPCs for information, including how to overcome barriers to training for particular groups. One LEPC actively supports SMEs in hiring new immigrants by demonstrating that it is in the employers' interest to recruit from this untapped talent pool. It goes on to connect them with language training and other services to support retention of new immigrant workers.

Policy makers rely on information. In order for the work of Future Skills and WICs to improve coverage and inclusiveness of adult learning beyond the testing context, policy makers and practitioners must have access to the evidence from programme evaluations and use it actively to improve programmes and policies. Dissemination approaches are discussed in the section below on impact of adult learning.

Box 2.7. Testing the United States' "Career Pathways" model in Ontario

The Career Pathways framework developed in the United States provides a model of post-secondary education and training delivery through a series of modular steps, with each step leading to higher credentials and employment opportunities. This model aligns education, workforce development and support services to support learners to attain high quality and sustainable employment. The components of a Career Pathway include accelerated credentials and placement, support services, employer engagement and subsidised cost of training programmes. A unique feature of this model is that the pathway has multiple entry and exit points, allowing individuals to enter at the most appropriate skill level and/or transition easily between participating in the labour market and pursuing further training. A review commissioned by the Department of Labor found that the health care sector most frequently implemented the Career Pathways model. Health care may be well suited to the Career Pathways model because there are clear occupational progressions, from entry-level (e.g. nursing aides, personal care aides), to mid-level (e.g. licensed and vocational nurses) to higher-level occupations (e.g. registered nurses, diagnostic-related technicians).

In Ontario, many lower-skilled adults find it difficult to access high quality jobs and employers struggle to find workers with the right skills. Recognising that the Career Pathways model has not been widely adopted outside the United States, the Ontario Centre for Workforce Innovation (OCWI) funded four projects focused on building the evidence base in Ontario. While none of the projects tested a fully developed Career Pathway, each project explored the development of some key features of the model.

The conclusion was that Career Pathways have the potential to meet skill needs in target sectors provided there is a deep understanding of the sector's skills needs. Strategic partnerships between employers, workforce development services, and education institutions are crucial for successful implementation. The assessment report concluded that future projects should focus on deepening partnerships with employers and labour market experts to identify sectors where the Career Pathways model could be effective.

Source: OCWI (2019[7]), "Career Pathways Demonstration Project Final Report"; https://ocwi-coie.ca/wp-content/uploads/2019/03/Career-Pathways-Demonstration-Project-Final-Report-March-11.pdf, Palamar, M. and K. Pasolli (2018[8]), "Career Pathways" a promising model for skills training, Institute for Research on Public Policy; https://policyoptions.irpp.org/magazines/november-2018/career-pathways-promising-model-skills-training/, Sarna, M. and J. Strawn (2018[9]), "Career Pathways Implementation Synthesis: Career Pathways Design Study", https://www.dol.gov/sites/dolgov/files/OASP/legacy/files/3-Career-Pathways-Implementation-Synthesis.pdf.

With a mandate to test approaches to reducing barriers to training and employment for under-represented groups, Future Skills and the NLWIC support broader coverage and inclusiveness in adult learning. They should continue to invest in flexible modes of adult learning delivery (e.g. online, distance, modular, part-time, evenings). This helps adults overcome time and cost barriers to training. Low-skilled adults, an under-represented group, could be a more explicit focus of the Future Skills and the NLWIC research programmes.

Recommendation 1: The Future Skills Center and WICs should test ways to engage low-skilled adults in learning.

Alignment of adult learning with labour market needs

One of the goals of adult learning is to improve a participant's labour market prospects. Doing so requires adults to develop skills that employers are asking for. Those skills are constantly changing. To facilitate the alignment of adult learning with changing labour market needs, programmes should respond to both current and future skill needs. Furthermore, adult learning programmes should specifically target those adults, both employed and unemployed, whose core skills risk obsolescence (OECD, 2019[6]).

Through their research agendas and priority setting, Future Skills and the WICs have the potential to improve the alignment of adult learning provision with labour market needs. The NLWIC prioritises proposals that have a skills development component and address current workforce challenges in priority sectors identified in the province's strategic vision document (i.e. tourism, forestry, and aquaculture, and others). It also prioritises research projects that enhance literacy and digital skills, as well as those that prepare individuals and industries for the "jobs of the future." In preparing their proposals, applicants must demonstrate that their specific training solution meets a labour market need, which requires applicants to research the labour market and consult with industry stakeholders. Future Skills establishes priorities based on ongoing engagement with labour market partners and stakeholders. The Future Skills Centre also works in close partnership with the Labour Market Information Council to identify in-demand skills and industry sector needs. Given its focus on preparing workers for future labour market trends, the Future Skills Centre and the WICs should exploit skills anticipation exercises (e.g. industry sector forecasts, the

Canadian Occupational Projection System, foresight exercises) in setting its research agenda. The WICs, on the other hand, should exploit assessments of current skill needs (e.g. employer surveys, sector studies, and surveys of workers or graduates).

Strong engagement with employers and industry is also key to ensuring that proposed training solutions align with employers' needs. The Future Skills Council engages industry stakeholders across sectors to build consensus on where Canada needs to focus its efforts to adapt to rapid change. Both the Future Skills Centre and the NLWIC encourage proposals from partnerships, including employers, employer groups, unions, training providers and other stakeholders. Sectoral or network approaches to employer engagement in designing training solutions have proven successful because they help SMEs to articulate common training needs. Further, they take advantage of economies of scale which reduces the time and cost burden on individual SMEs. There are several examples of effective sectoral or network approaches to training solutions both in Canada and internationally. Under the Sectoral Initiatives programme, key sectors of the Canadian economy receive support to address current and future skills shortages through the development of sector-specific labour market intelligence, national occupational standards, and skills certification and accreditation systems. A recent evaluation found that they have been successful in their mandate, but that efforts to disseminate findings could be strengthened (ESDC, 2018[10]). In England, the Employer Ownership of Skills Pilot funded employer-led partnerships to find innovative ways to address skills development and workplace productivity. An evaluation found that this network model reduced risks and costs for individual employers by pooling learners across SMEs (Box 2.10). A similar programme in the United Kingdom targeted sector skills councils (Employment Investment Fund, Box 2.10). The Irish Skillnet model offers business owners a learning network of businesses in the same sector and empowers them to determine their training needs and coordinate the delivery of training.

Another way to improve the alignment between training provision and labour market needs is by specifically targeting those adults whose core skills are or will likely become obsolete. Most of the selected projects of the Future Skills Centre and half of the NLWIC projects focus on retraining workers and jobseekers for jobs in high-demand sectors. These projects upskill or retrain workers who are at high risk of displacement due to technological change. For instance, the Future Skills Centre tests an approach to equip workers in retail and meat processing (both sectors that are facing large-scale displacement of workers due to automation) with the requisite skills, trade certifications and professional standards to transition to industries and roles with projected growth (e.g. chefs, cooks, bakers, retail sales supervisor, horticultural technicians and accommodation service managers). Similarly, the NLWIC tests an approach to retrain workers and jobseekers from non-tourism sectors to support a growing tourism sector in rural Newfoundland (Box 2.4). An important difference is that the WICs mostly address immediate labour market needs whereas the Future Skills Centre looks at how to prepare workers for future realities.

Through their research and engagement efforts, Future Skills and WICs have the potential to improve the alignment of adult learning provision with labour market needs. Many of the selected projects of the Future Skills Centre and the NLWIC focus on retraining workers and jobseekers for jobs in high-demand sectors and/or upskilling or retraining workers who are at risk of displacement due to technological change. The Future Skills Council supports collaboration across sectors to identify priority areas for action to ensure Canada has a skilled workforce. The Future Skills Centre and the WICs should continue to encourage proposals from employer groups and other industry partnerships.

Recommendation 2: Future Skills and the WICs should exploit assessments and forecasts of skills needs in setting their priorities and research agendas.

Impact of adult learning

For job-related training to have a positive impact on labour market outcomes, training must be of high quality and relate closely to skills needed by employers. An enabling environment at the workplace is also essential to put acquired skills to good use. Finally, reliable information about the quality and outcomes of training programmes should be gathered and circulated. Such information helps individuals, employers and public employment services make sound investments in adult learning.

In Canada, reliable information about the quality of training programmes could be improved. A review of the existing evidence base called for "systematic, independent, academic evaluations that use randomised controlled trials" in evaluating the outcomes of training programmes (Jansen et al., 2019[11]).

All projects funded by the Future Skills Centre are required to undergo an independent evaluation that must abide by an evaluation framework. The evaluation framework ensures consistency in evaluation practices and enables comparison between projects. The Future Skills Centre is also working with Statistics Canada to track the medium-term impact of its projects. If findings from these evaluations are disseminated well, this can help to build an evidence base about the outcomes of training programmes. By identifying approaches that work, this evidence can then inform to the direction of investments in existing adult learning programmes and make the case for new investments and improvements to programmes.

While NLWIC applicants are required to demonstrate with evidence that their project addresses a labour market need, projects are not required to undergo a formal evaluation. Funded projects may evaluate existing programmes that have not yet been evaluated, but evaluation is not a requirement for most projects. A key challenge identified by focus group participants was that many community organisations receiving funding to test a new approach do not have the capacity to carry out their own evaluation or manage an evaluation process. They could benefit from support in learning how to share the results of their project in the framework of an evaluation or otherwise. To build this capacity, the NLWIC is considering offering seminars or online resources on how to apply for grants and prepare evaluation guides.

Some countries with similar programmes require that grantees carry out their own evaluations or hire independent evaluators. For instance, grantees of the United States' Workforce Innovation Fund must hire independent evaluators to examine and report on their interventions. To support grantees, the United States Department of Labor offers online guides and webinars through its WorkforceGPS website on how to prepare an evaluation plan and how to choose an evaluator (Box 2.8).

Other programmes match projects with independent evaluators. This has the advantage of reducing the burden on grantees who may not have the internal capacity to prepare an evaluation plan or hire and manage the work of an external evaluator. As a requirement of annual funding under the National Training Fund, Skillnet Ireland employs external consultants to conduct annual independent evaluations of their sectoral training programmes that cover their inputs, activities, and outcomes.

Evaluating projects based on common outcome indicators enables comparison of performance. Analysis from Laboissiere and Moursed (2017[12]) based on evidence from the United States emphasises the importance of collecting outcome data that enables a calculation of the return on investment (ROI) of a particular project. Employers are more likely to participate and pay for workforce development programmes if they have proof of ROI. They suggest tracking the cost of programme recruitment and training, employer productivity and quality outcomes, retention and speed to promotion (Laboissiere and Mourshed, 2017[12]). To measure the impact on individuals, important metrics include comparison of income of graduates before and after training, continued employment, job promotion and reliance on public support.

The Future Skills Centre and WICs have the potential to contribute to a stronger impact evaluation culture in Canada. The main difference between monitoring outcomes and a real impact evaluation is the use of a counterfactual to estimate what part of the observed outcomes can be attributed to the training intervention (White, Sinha and Flanagan, 2006[13]). An impact evaluation of an adult learning programme generally compares the outcomes of training participants to the outcomes of similar adults who did not participate. The centres that make up the UK What Works Network use a variety of standards of evidence to assess the robustness of impact evaluations. These include the five-point Scientific Maryland Scale (SMS) (Table 2.4) used by the What Works Centre for Local Economic Growth. Under the SMS, Level 5 is reserved for randomised control trials. The Centre prioritises impact evaluations that have the potential to score three or above on the SMS when assessing the evidence base.

Table 2.4. The Scientific Maryland Scale

	Characteristics of impact evaluation
Level 1	Correlation of outcomes with presence or intensity of treatment, cross-sectional comparisons of treated groups with untreated groups, or other cross-sectional methods in which there is no attempt to establish a counterfactual.
Level 2	Comparison of outcomes in treated group after an intervention, with outcomes in the treated group before the intervention ('before and after' study).
Level 3	Comparison of outcomes in treated group after an intervention, with outcomes in the treated group before the intervention, and a comparison group used to provide a counterfactual (e.g. difference in difference). Evidence presented on comparability of treatment and control groups but they are poorly balanced on pre-treatment characteristics.
Level 4	Comparison of outcomes in treated group after an intervention, with outcomes in the treated group before the intervention, and a comparison group used to provide a counterfactual (i.e. difference in difference). Evidence presented on comparability of treatment and control groups and they are balanced on pre-treatment characteristics.
Level 5	Reserved for research designs that involve randomisation into treatment and control groups.

Source: What Works Centre for Local Economic Growth, "About our reviews", https://whatworksgrowth.org/public/files/Methodology/14-03-20_About_our_Reviews.pdf.

A key challenge in developing evidence on the impact of training programmes is tracking participants long enough to observe measurable impact. Many of the indicators noted above entail several years of observation. With project funding lasting two or three years, there is often insufficient time to assess factors beyond the initial programme implementation and any short-term impacts (i.e. less than a year). Importantly, a meta-analysis of active labour market programmes (Card, Kluve and Weber, 2018[14]) found that classroom and on-the-job training programmes for the unemployed have a positive impact on employment in the medium term (i.e. after two years). In the short term, though, the impact is insignificant or even negative due to "lock in effects" (i.e. training participants suspend job search effort while training). With the investment fund programmes in the United Kingdom that funded skills infrastructure projects, the final evaluation concluded that a longer timeframe than two years after engagement was needed, and that training impacts may take up to seven years to materialise (Tu et al., 2016[15]). One way to track programme participants for longer periods is by linking information about the same person from two or more data sources (e.g. survey and administrative data). But there are caveats associated with data linkage, notably the challenges with protecting individual confidentiality. The Education and Labour Market Longitudinal Linkage Platform, announced in Canada's 2019 federal budget[2], supports data linkage efforts that preserve confidentiality by replacing personal identifiers with linkage keys.

Backlash can follow public investment in workforce innovation if tested approaches prove unsuccessful. Fear that a programme will be shut down unless funded projects are successful could create incentives for biased evaluations, undermining a better understanding about what works. To combat this, and to promote a culture of rigorous evaluation, the Future Skills Centre and WICs should challenge themselves to highlight the evaluation results both from successful and unsuccessful projects. Knowing what does not work when it comes to training and upskilling adults is just as important as knowing what does work. The What Works Network in the United Kingdom has adopted this approach. In their 5-year report, they draw attention to both the types of interventions that did not have expected impacts, as well as those that did. Somewhat counter-intuitively, one What Works Centre found that re-training workers post-employment appears to have a more positive effect on employment rates and earnings than traditional outplacement services provided before the workers leave their existing jobs (What Works Centre, 2018[16]).

Disseminating the evidence from evaluations in accessible ways facilitates its use among practitioners of adult learning. They can then modify programmes for better performance. For instance, the BC Centre for Employment Excellence introduced a webinar and a podcast series, *Innovate, Implement and Inspire*, which explored uncommon approaches to labour market challenges and featured interviews with practitioners. Lessons learned from projects funded by the United States' Workforce Innovation Fund are published online as case studies. In Victoria, Australia, the inaugural Workforce Training Innovation Fund showcase held at the Melbourne Convention Centre in 2019 highlighted the results gathered from twelve funded projects that delivered novel training approaches. Skillnet Ireland created an online video bank to showcase the impact of its training initiatives. In the United Kingdom, Unionlearn set up a blog where employers can share their experiences, advice and insights about the impact of workforce development initiatives based on evaluations.

Policy makers can also use evidence from evaluations to improve the quality of programmes at the national level. Evaluations from the United States' WIF played a key role in informing the passage of the Workforce Innovation and Opportunity Act (WIOA) in 2014, which replaced the Workforce Investment Act (WIA) (Betesh, 2017[17]). WIOA places more emphasis on the use of evidence-based programming in workforce development policy. The legislation prioritises successful approaches tested under WIF. For example, one WIF project found that offering accelerated career pathways training in manufacturing increased employment rates and quarterly earnings for programme participants relative to a control group (Betesh et al., 2017[18]). The WIOA now emphasises both career pathways and sector strategies in the delivery of workforce development services. In Canada, the Future Skills Office within ESDC was created to ensure the findings from the Council and the Centre are considered by all governments (federal, provincial, territorial) when developing and investing in new programmes.

An important policy action is to synthesise the body of existing evidence so that it is accessible for policy makers and practitioners. The UK What Works Centres perform a useful service in this regard by establishing an agreed set of standards for assessing the quality of evaluations, distilling existing evidence into concrete guidance for policy makers, and filling gaps in the evidence base by commissioning new trials (Box 2.9).

Fostering better use of newly acquired skills in the workplace also encourages higher returns on training. This is still an undeveloped policy area in Canada. Some countries have undertaken initiatives from which Canada can learn. Chapter 3 will discuss ways that the research activities of the WICs and Future Skills could build an evidence base around effective workplace practices that foster better use of skills.

Box 2.8. United States' Workforce Innovation Fund and WorkforceGPS

Workforce Innovation Fund

The Department of Labor's Workforce Innovation Fund (WIF) supports innovation in workforce development at the systems and service delivery levels. Since 2012, the WIF has provided 45 competitive grants to states, regions, and localities to transform the public workforce system, including breaking down programme silos and implementing innovative approaches to the design and delivery of employment and training services. The Department of Labor finances the WIF to invest in programmes that support, evaluate and enhance workforce investment strategies, particularly for vulnerable populations, youth and dislocated workers.

Each grantee must commission its own independent evaluation. The Employment and Training Administration hired a National Evaluation Coordinator (NEC) to oversee the independent evaluations commissioned by WIF grantees. The NEC provides each grantee with support to ensure that they meet the evaluation requirements and to help them secure third-party evaluators. The NEC also assists the evaluators in complying with evaluation requirements.

WorkforceGPS

Funded by the Department of Labor, WorkforceGPS is an online portal that provides technical assistance for workforce professionals, educators and business leaders. Training materials and online learning resources on evaluation design and implementation are available on the website. An evaluation toolkit provides information about choosing an evaluation model and selecting appropriate third-party evaluators, such as higher education institutions or research firms. For instance, they note that collaborating with research universities to conduct evaluations has advantages: universities often have access to "big data" computing facilities and evaluations can serve as research opportunities for graduate students, which may entail less cost than with private firms or in-house services. The Evaluation Hub Peer Learning Cohort Forum provides an interactive platform for participants to discuss challenges and solutions in evaluation design and implementation.

Source: U.S. Department of Labor, Employment and Training Administration (2018[19]), Evaluation Toolkit: Key Elements for State Workforce Agencies; WorkforceGPS, "About WorkforceGPS", https://innovation.workforcegps.org/about.

Box 2.9. What Works Network in the United Kingdom

The What Works Network was launched in the United Kingdom in 2013, and now consists of 13 What Works Centres. The Centres are independent from one another, operating with different levels of funding and areas of focus such as policing, education, youth unemployment, local economic growth, and health and social care. Each Centre is committed to generating evidence, translating that evidence into relevant and actionable guidance, and helping decision makers take action.

One of the core functions of the What Works Centres is to help practitioners reach judgments by producing assessments of the quality of existing evidence in their field of expertise. The Centres screen evaluations based on the robustness of their research methods, with those using randomised control trials scoring the highest. Of the over 3 000 studies on adult learning identified by the What Works Centre for Well-being, only 25 met robustness standards. The assessments also summarise for policy makers the types of interventions that work, for whom and under which circumstances.

The Centres help to fill gaps in the evidence base by calling attention to those gaps, directly commissioning research, and building the capacity of local and national policymakers and practitioners to generate high-quality evidence. For instance, the What Works Centre for Well-being runs an annual course for civil servants on how to incorporate well-being into policy analysis and has developed a micro-site to help charities evaluate whether their activities improve the well-being of the people they support.

A particularly important role of the Centres is to translate evidence into guidance. Recognising that practitioners and front-line workers have little time to read lengthy evidence reviews, the Centres translate their assessments into short, practical manuals that break down key information into steps. They also disseminate guidance via digital media, and through outreach programmes including practitioner academies, local partnerships, and master classes.

Source: What Works Network (2018[20]), "The What Works Network Five Years On", www.gov.uk/guidance/what-works-network ; Work Works Centre for Local Economic Growth, "About our reviews", https://whatworksgrowth.org/public/files/Methodology/14-03-20_About_our_Reviews.pdf.

All projects funded by the Future Skills Centre are required to undergo an evaluation. Projects funded by the NLWIC are not subject to an evaluation requirement and grantees lack capacity to carry out evaluations on their own.

Recommendation 3: WICs should build the capacity of grantees to monitor the impact of their projects.

Recommendation 4: The Future Skills Centre should establish quality standards for evaluations to improve the impact evaluation culture in Canada, possibly following the Scientific Maryland Scale.

Recommendation 5: The Future Skills Centre and WICs should allocate sufficient funding to track participants' outcomes from training-related projects over the longer term (i.e. 2-3 years after implementation). This is already part of the Future Skills Centre mandate. The Government of Canada should also support data linkage efforts that enable researchers and policy makers to track training participant outcomes over the long-term.

Recommendation 6: Future Skills and WICs should draw inspiration from international efforts to strengthen their planned dissemination efforts, including webinars, in-person showcases, conferences, master classes, and policy briefs.

Financing

The Future Skills Centre and WICs together allocate a substantial public investment towards adult learning through their competitive grants. These grants are not intended to finance the delivery of adult learning. Rather, they are used to prototype and evaluate innovative models of skills development.

The work of Future Skills and the WICs can improve the financing of Canada's adult learning system in two ways. First, it can bring to light innovative but cost-effective models of skills development. Second, it can encourage the development of co-financing partnerships.

In Canada, the financial cost of training represents a barrier to participation for individuals. According to the OECD Survey of Adult Skills, 19% of adults in Canada who wanted to participate more in training did not do so because it was too expensive (see Chapter 1). This is higher than the OECD average (16%) and is the second most reported barrier for individuals after being too busy at work. In evaluating innovative approaches to skills development, one element of the evaluation framework should be whether the training can be delivered in a way that is affordable for the individual and/or employer.

An effective financing model for adult learning entails a sufficient level of funding provided through a mix of co-financing by government, employers and individuals. Encouraging co-financing arrangements through the projects they support is one way that Future Skills and the WICs can help overcome financial constraints to training. Under current rules, the Future Skills Centre encourages but does not require in-kind matching contributions from successful applicants. Neither does the NLWIC impose any matching requirements on applicants. Some countries with similar programmes require that applicants match the grant with their own contributions, which can induce a greater stake in the project, leading to stronger ownership. At the same time, matching requirements may limit the participation of SMEs who face greater time and cost constraints. The United Kingdom Commission for Employment and Skills (UKCES) piloted a series of co-investment funds between 2011 and 2016 (Box 2.10). Employers were eligible to propose solutions to skills challenges and successful employers were required to match the investment with their own contribution. An impact evaluation found that the programmes were successful at improving engagement of employers in training, but that SME engagement remained low. Requiring a lower contribution from SMEs is one way to overcome this challenge. In Australia, the Industry Skills Fund targeted growth-oriented SMEs and operated under a co-financing model with the firm's contribution based on a sliding scale depending on the size and location of the firm. An impact evaluation based on survey evidence found that 42% of businesses would not have conducted training in the absence of the fund, suggesting that it was successful in encouraging small businesses to provide training where they otherwise would not have (ACIL Allen Consulting, 2016[21]).

Box 2.10. United Kingdom Commission for Employment and Skills

Pilot co-investment funds to support innovative and demand-led skills solutions

Between 2011 and 2016, the UKCES piloted a series of investment fund programmes to incentivise a demand-led approach to skills development. These pilot funds included the *Employer Investment Fund* (launched in 2011, supported 87 projects), the *Growth and Innovation Fund* (launched in 2011, supported 37 projects), the *Employer Ownership of Skills* initiative (2012-2014), and the *UK Futures Programme* (2014-16).

The Employment Investment Fund (EIF) and the Growth and Innovation Fund (GIF) made time-limited funding available for start-up investments in skills and employment infrastructure, with no participation funding available (i.e. no direct funding for the training of specific individuals). Eligibility for EIF was restricted to sector skills councils, while eligibility for GIF was not. Co-funding of projects was mandatory: the UKCES invested GBP 111 million in 124 projects under the EIF and GIF, and employers matched an additional GBP 103 million. The impact evaluation for these two funds noted that they successfully engaged employers, particularly in sectors with strong supply chains and peer networks (like advanced manufacturing and energy and utilities), but SME engagement remained low. Where SME engagement was successful, strategies included use of specialist brokers with sectoral knowledge as well as face-to-face communication to ensure that the offer met the specific needs of SMEs and to encourage take-up. The investments from EIF and GIF resulted in new online skills diagnostic tools, networks/partnerships and the development of training capacity. However, only one in five projects was expected to be financially sustainable after the initial public investment was spent.

The Employer Ownership of Skills Pilot (EOP) in England funded employer-led partnerships to find innovative ways to address skills development and workplace productivity. Through a competitive bidding process, companies could submit proposals that focused on industrial partnerships with employee representative groups. Employers were encouraged to work together with training providers, trade unions and other relevant actors, to develop their own skills agenda and drive the design and delivery of skills solutions for their workers. Investment funds could support leadership and management training for SMEs and social enterprises. An intermediate evaluation of the programme concluded that the EOP resulted in SMEs providing training that they would not have otherwise. The key element was found to be the collaborative model used by the EOP, which reduced risks and costs for individual employers by pooling learners across SMEs.

Under the *UK Futures Programme* (UKFP), the UKCES offered public co-investment to employers and industry to design and test their own solutions to emerging or long-standing skills and productivity challenges. The UKFP set five "productivity challenges," including addressing skills shortages in the off-site construction sector, enhancing skills for innovation management and commercialisation in the manufacturing sector, and developing progression pathways in the hospitality and retail sectors. Employer engagement was most effective when utilising existing networks (e.g. sector bodies) and engaging in face-to-face conversations.

Source: BIS (2015[22]), "Evaluation of the Employer Ownership of Skills Pilot, Round 1: Initial findings", Department for Business, Innovation and Skills, https://assets.publishing.service.gov.uk/government/uploads/system/uploads/attachment_data/file/412685/BIS-15-178-evaluation-of-the-employer-ownership-of-skills-pilot-round-1.pdf; OECD (2017[23]) Getting Skills Right: United Kingdom, https://dx.doi.org/10.1787/9789264280489-en; Tu et al. (2016[15]), "Employer Investment Fund (EIF) and Growth and Innovation Fund (GIF) Programme Level Evaluation: Final Report", https://www.gov.uk/government/publications/employer-investment-fund-and-growth-and-innovation-fund-programme-level-evaluation; UKCES (2015[24]), "Impact evaluation of the Employer Investment Fund and Growth Innovation Fund: project level learning and performance", https://assets.publishing.service.gov.uk/government/uploads/system/uploads/attachment_data/file/417738/Review_final_for_web.pdf; UKCES (2011[25]), "Employer Ownership of Skills: Securing a sustainable partnership for the long term, UK Commission for Employment and Skills", https://assets.publishing.service.gov.uk/government/uploads/system/uploads/attachment_data/file/305746/employer-ownership-of-skills-web-vision-report-final2.pdf.

The Future Skills Centre and WICs direct substantial public investment to testing innovative approaches to skill development.

Recommendation 7: The Future Skills Centre and WICs could further stimulate co-financed adult learning solutions by requiring that successful applicants match contributions, possibly on a sliding scale so that smaller firms contribute less than larger firms do.

Governance and co-ordination

Adult learning in Canada, as in other countries, comprises a complex policy field with programmes designed for a variety of objectives and target groups. With responsibility for adult learning split across ministries, levels of government, and often shared with social partners, training providers, or NGOs, strong coordination mechanisms are essential. OECD (2003[26]) called for a co-ordinated approach to adult learning whereby there is "a balanced interaction between a top-down approach – in which governments define structures and financing procedures – and a bottom-up approach that enables local actors to provide feedback on the problems they face and the innovative solutions they have found".

The new skills-related programmes in Canada support a balance between a top-down and bottom-up approach to workforce innovation and adult learning. Policy responses can be challenging in a federal model where provinces and territories have responsibility for education and training policy. Future Skills has the potential to improve coordination on adult learning policy in Canada. The design of Future Skills is intended to ensure that evidence generated by the Future Skills Centre and Council is disseminated across all governments and to networks of stakeholders. This is achieved by the Future Skills Office engaging with other federal government departments and the provinces and territories to support the integration of evidence into policy and programme design. The independence of the Future Skills Centre may also support coordination efforts. An independent and well-reputed organisation conducting skill assessment and anticipation exercises can facilitate social dialogue about skills needs, as has been the case in Belgium (Flanders), Norway, the United Kingdom and Australia. Balance is essential. While national leadership supports a coordinated top-down approach, the diverse economic and cultural conditions across provinces and territories in Canada justify a regional approach to workforce development. The WICs and LEPCs support such an approach.

Stakeholder engagement is a stated priority for Future Skills, the NLWIC, and the LEPCs. Examples of how to continue to engage stakeholders can be drawn from the experience of Australia's Try, Test and Learn Fund, in which the Department of Social Services carried out a variety of consultations with stakeholders, including design workshops, early consultations with states and territory governments, and a policy hack to discuss lessons learned (Box 2.11).

The research agendas of the Future Skills Centre and the WICs present an opportunity to improve cooperation between stakeholders in the policy response to changing skills needs. By encouraging proposals from partnerships of employer groups, unions, training institutions, practitioners and other community actors, the Future Skills Centre and the WICs can facilitate coordinated solutions to skills challenges. This is similar to the approach taken in the United States, where the Department of Labor awards competitive Workforce Innovation Fund grants to consortia of state workforce agencies or local workforce investment boards to implement new or untested approaches to workforce development.

The involvement of the provinces and territories in the development and management of Future Skills deserves careful thought, particularly given that five provinces have established their own WICs with similar mandates to the Future Skills Centre. The Mowat Centre argues that "the Future Skills Centre should be seen … as an experiment in the development of a more mature approach to federal-provincial institutional co-governance in Canada" (Parkin, Hartmann and Morden, 2017[27]), and that it ought to be jointly created, owned and managed by all 14 governments (10 provinces, 3 territories, federal government). Future Skills works with the Forum of Labour Market Ministers to support involvement of provinces and territories. This collaboration helps to align priorities, ensure complimentary efforts and share knowledge. While the provinces are not currently involved in the governance of the Future Skills Centre, the Centre holds bilateral discussions with provinces and territories. The Centre is also working with provinces and territories to identify how to have a presence in each region to address regional needs. The Future Skills Centre can foster further dialogue and coordination between the provincial WICs, for instance, through national conferences, promotion of joint projects, and by acting as a repository of good practice.

Box 2.11. Australia's Try, Test and Learn Fund

Launched in 2016 and managed by the Department of Social Services, Australia's Try, Test and Learn Fund tests innovative approaches to assist groups of people at risk of long-term welfare dependence. Two separate "tranches" or calls for proposals were carried out as part of the programme, with AUD 96.1 million allocated towards 53 projects. The programme itself is currently under evaluation.

The open and collaborative approach to policy development is a key strength of the Try, Test and Learn Fund. Recognising the importance of stakeholder engagement, the Department of Social Services reached out to representatives from the community sector, business, academia and the general public in the following ways:

- A consultative design workshop to seek stakeholders' inputs on the fund
- Consultations with state and territory governments
- A policy hack on lessons learned from the first tranche
- An ideas exchange with employers, community leaders and service providers
- Information sessions across Australia to spread awareness of the fund for potential tranche two applicants

Source: Department of Social Services (2019[28]), Stakeholder engagement: Try, Test and Learn fund., https://www.dss.gov.au/review-of-australias-welfare-system/australian-priority-investment-approach-to-welfare/stakeholder-engagement.

The combination of Future Skills, provincial WICs, and local actors (including Ontario's Local Employment Planning Councils) supports a balance between a top-down and bottom-up approach to workforce innovation and adult learning. As an independent body, the Future Skills Centre can facilitate better coordination on workforce innovation and adult learning policy in Canada.

Recommendation 8: The Future Skills Centre should play a leadership role in coordinating dialogue between the WICs, through national conferences, facilitating joint projects, and acting as a repository of good practice.

Assessment and recommendations

Overall, Canada's new workforce innovation programmes stand to improve the future-readiness of the adult learning system in a substantive way. Suggested areas for improvement are summarised in the table below.

Most of the initiatives supported by Future Skills and the WICs focus on the supply side of the labour market (e.g. skills development, matching jobseekers with jobs, reducing barriers for under-represented groups). But the demand side of workforce development – creating opportunities for learning and development within firms – is equally important. An enabling workplace environment amplifies the returns to adult learning by creating opportunities for adults to apply their newly acquired skills. The next chapter introduces the concept of learning organisations, and the role of high-performance work practices in contributing to better skills use and learning within the workplace. It highlights examples of how countries promote such practices within firms, and suggests how Canada could stimulate and promote such practices.

Recommendations

The following actions should be taken by Future Skills and the provincial workforce innovation centers:

Coverage and inclusiveness

- Test ways to engage low-skilled adults in learning.

Alignment of training with labour market needs

- Exploit assessments and forecasts of skill needs in setting their priorities and research agendas.

Impact of adult learning

- Build the capacity of grantees to monitor the impact of their projects.
- Establish quality standards through the Future Skills Center to improve the impact evaluation culture in Canada, possibly following the Scientific Maryland Scale.
- Allocate sufficient funding to track participants' outcomes from training-related projects over the longer term (i.e. 2-3 years after implementation). This is already part of the Future Skills Centre mandate. The Canadian government should also support data linkage efforts that enable researchers and policy makers to track training participant outcomes over the long-term.
- Draw inspiration from international efforts to strengthen planned dissemination efforts, including webinars, in-person showcases, conferences and policy briefs.

Financing

- Stimulate further co-financed adult learning solutions by requiring that successful applicants match contributions, possibly on a sliding scale so that smaller firms contribute less than larger firms do.

Governance and co-ordination

- Under the leadership of the Future Skills Centre, coordinate dialogue between the WICs, through national conferences, facilitating joint projects, and building a repository of good practice.

References

ACIL Allen Consulting (2016), "Industry Skills Fund and the Youth Stream Pilot Programs: Independent Evaluation Final Report".   [21]

Betesh, H. (2017), *Evidence in Action: Connecting Workforce Innovation Fund Evaluation Results to the Implementation of WIOA*, Social Policy Research Associates, https://www.spra.com/2017/06/28/evidence-in-action/.   [17]

Betesh, H. et al. (2017), *Evaluation of Accelerated Training for Illinois Manufacturing (ATIM) Impact Report*, Social Policy Research Associates.   [18]

BIS (2015), *Evaluation of the Employer Ownership of Skills Pilot, Round 1: Initial findings*, Department for Business, Innovation and Skills, https://assets.publishing.service.gov.uk/government/uploads/system/uploads/attachment_data/file/412685/BIS-15-178-evaluation-of-the-employer-ownership-of-skills-pilot-round-1.pdf.   [22]

Card, D., J. Kluve and A. Weber (2018), "What Works? A Meta Analysis of Recent Active Labor Market Program Evaluations", *Journal of the European Economic Association*, Vol. 16/3, pp. 894-931, http://dx.doi.org/10.1093/jeea/jvx028.   [14]

Department of Social Services (2019), *Stakeholder engagement: Try, test and learn fund*, https://www.dss.gov.au/review-of-australias-welfare-system/australian-priority-investment-approach-to-welfare/stakeholder-engagement.   [28]

ESDC (2018), "Evaluation of the Sectoral Initiatives Program", https://www.canada.ca/en/employment-social-development/corporate/reports/evaluations/sectoral-initiatives-program.html.   [10]

Government of Ontario (2018), *Local Employment Planning Councils (LEPC)*, http://www.tcu.gov.on.ca/eng/eopg/programs/lepc.html.   [4]

Jacobs, R. and J. Hawley (2009), "The Emergence of 'Workforce Development': Definition, Conceptual Boundaries and Implications", in *International Handbook of Education for the Changing World of Work*, Springer Netherlands, http://dx.doi.org/10.1007/978-1-4020-5281-1_167.   [3]

Jansen, A. et al. (2019), "Training and Skills Development Policy Options for the Changing World of Work", *Canadian Public Policy*, Vol. December, pp. 460-482, http://dx.doi.org/10.3131/cpp.2019-024.   [11]

Laboissiere, M. and M. Mourshed (2017), *Closing the skills gap: Creating workforce-development programs that work for everyone*, McKinsey & Company, https://www.mckinsey.com/industries/social-sector/our-insights/closing-the-skills-gap-creating-workforce-development-programs-that-work-for-everyone#.   [12]

McDougall, A. (2019), "All Together Now: Intergovernmental Relations in Canada's Labour Market Sector", IRPP Study 75. Montreal: Institute for Research on Public Policy, https://doi.org/10.26070/xa9d-r145.   [29]

OCWI (2019), *Career Pathways Demonstration Project Final Report*, https://ocwi-coie.ca/wp-content/uploads/2019/03/Career-Pathways-Demonstration-Project-Final-Report-March-11.pdf. [7]

OECD (2019), "Getting Skills Right: Engaging low-skilled adults in learning", Organisation for Economic Cooperation and Development, Paris, http://www.oecd.org/employment/emp/engaging-low-skilled-adults-2019.pdf. [6]

OECD (2019), *Getting Skills Right: Future-Ready Adult Learning Systems*, Getting Skills Right, OECD Publishing, Paris, https://dx.doi.org/10.1787/9789264311756-en. [1]

OECD (2017), *Getting Skills Right: United Kingdom*, Getting Skills Right, OECD Publishing, Paris, https://dx.doi.org/10.1787/9789264280489-en. [23]

OECD (2003), *Beyond Rhetoric: Adult Learning Policies and Practices*, OECD Publishing, Paris, https://dx.doi.org/10.1787/9789264199446-en. [26]

Palamar, M. and K. Pasolli (2018), *"Career Pathways" a promising model for skills training*, Institute for Research on Public Policy, https://policyoptions.irpp.org/magazines/november-2018/career-pathways-promising-model-skills-training/. [8]

Parkin, A., E. Hartmann and M. Morden (2017), *How to Build a Skills Lab: A new model of institutional governance in Canada*. [27]

Sarna, M. and J. Strawn (2018), *Career Pathways Implementation Synthesis Career Pathways Design Study*, https://www.dol.gov/sites/dolgov/files/OASP/legacy/files/3-Career-Pathways-Implementation-Synthesis.pdf. [9]

Tu, T. et al. (2016), *Employer Investment Fund (EIF) and Growth and Innovation Fund (GIF) Programme Level Evaluation: Final report*, UK Commission for Employment and Skills, https://www.gov.uk/government/publications/employer-investment-fund-and-growth-and-innovation-fund-programme-level-evaluation (accessed on 19 December 2019). [15]

U.S. Department of Labor (2018), *Evaluation Toolkit: Key Elements for State Workforce Agencies*, https://evalhub.workforcegps.org/resources/2018/09/07/19/58/WIOA-Evaluation-Toolkit. [19]

UKCES (2015), "Impact evaluation of the Employer Investment Fund and Growth and Innovation Fund: project level learning and performance", UK Commission for Employment and Skills, https://assets.publishing.service.gov.uk/government/uploads/system/uploads/attachment_data/file/417738/Review_final_for_web.pdf (accessed on 19 December 2019). [24]

UKCES (2011), *Employer Ownership of Skills: Securing a sustainable partnership for the long term*, UK Commission for Employment and Skills, https://assets.publishing.service.gov.uk/government/uploads/system/uploads/attachment_data/file/305746/employer-ownership-of-skills-web-vision-report-final2.pdf. [25]

What Works Centre (2018), *Toolkit: Responding to major job losses*, https://whatworksgrowth.org/resources/toolkit-responding-to-major-job-losses/. [16]

What Works Network (2018), *The What Works Network - Five Years On*, https://assets.publishing.service.gov.uk/government/uploads/system/uploads/attachment_data/file/677478/6.4154_What_works_report_Final.pdf. [20]

White, H., S. Sinha and A. Flanagan (2006), *A review of the state of impact evaluation*, http://www.oecd.org/development/evaluation/dcdndep/37634226.pdf. [13]

Windisch, H. (2015), "Adults with low literacy and numeracy skills: A literature review on policy intervention", *OECD Education Working Papers*, No. 123, OECD Publishing, Paris, https://dx.doi.org/10.1787/5jrxnjdd3r5k-en. [5]

Zizys, T. (2018), *Workforce development, demand-led strategies and the goal of good jobs.*, Prepared for: Ontario Centre for Workforce Innovation, https://ocwi-coie.ca/wp-content/uploads/2018/08/01-018-01-Zizys-Tom-Final-Report.pdf (accessed on 29 August 2019). [2]

Notes

[1] The Ontario Centre for Workforce Innovation was initiated in 2015 and closed in 2019 due to a provincial level decision to end funding.

[2] https://crdcn.org/article/education-and-labour-market-longitudinal-linkage-platform.

3 Promoting skills use and learning organisations

There is evidence that the way work is organised, jobs are designed and employees are managed matter for turning workplaces into learning organisations where employees are encouraged to apply and develop their skills. There are advantages for both employees and employers. Nevertheless, work practices that encourage skills use and promote the development of learning organisations are not widespread. This chapter reviews international experience with promoting high-performance work practices, and suggests how Canada could stimulate good practice in this area.

Introduction

A positive learning environment in the workplace can stimulate participation in training, raise returns on training and encourage deployment of skills. As discussed in Chapter 1, greater skills use leads to higher employee satisfaction and productivity. Adults working in organisations with strong learning cultures are better able to adapt to the changing demand for skills, and their employers in turn benefit from this edge.

Governments generally prefer to leave what happens within a firm – how work is organised, jobs are designed and people are managed – to employers. They tend to focus on supply side policies like education and training policy, rather than attempting to influence the way skills are used and developed internally within the workplace. Yet recognising the influence of positive learning environments within workplaces, several countries have undertaken "workplace innovation" programmes with a view to building the evidence base, raising awareness and funding interventions at the workplace level.

Given Canada's tight labour market, growing skills shortages and modest record on productivity, efforts to promote skills use and learning within workplaces seem of value. Canada could consider introducing a programme to support the use and development of the existing skills supply. While Canada does not yet have a workplace innovation programme, the mandate of the workforce innovation centres and Future Skills could make them ideal bodies to take up the role of promoting good practice in this area in Canada.

This chapter starts by defining a "learning organisation". It introduces the concept of "high performance work practices" (HPWP) and reviews evidence showing their link to higher skills use, informal learning and training participation. It outlines trends in the use of HPWP, and considers obstacles to their wider adoption. The chapter then reviews international models of workplace innovation programmes. It discusses their policy focus, governance, financing and monitoring. A potential strategy for Canada in developing its own workplace innovation programme is laid out.

Defining learning organisations

A learning organisation is one with a capacity to adapt and to compete through learning (OECD, 2010[1]). Much of the literature on learning organisations is concerned with the promotion of human resource management policies that are supportive of learning cultures. This includes opportunities for upskilling, but also performance assessment, skill-based compensation, transparent career paths, supportive management and opportunities for informal learning (Johnston and Hawke, 2002[2]; OECD, 2010[1]). Work organisation and management practices that reward and facilitate the application of new skills complement skill development. They amplify the returns to learning. The Australian Workforce and Productivity Agency outlined a number of work organisation practices linked to the enhanced use of skills (Box 3.1).

The term "high performance work practices" refers to a set of human resources practices that are shown to be associated with greater skills use and informal learning. HPWPs include aspects of work organisation and job design such as teamwork, autonomy, task discretion, mentoring, job rotation, and applying new learning. They also deal with management practices such as employee participation, incentive pay, training practices and flexibility in working hours (OECD, 2016[3]). Other terms are often used synonymously with HPWP, including workplace innovation, innovative workplaces, high-involvement or high-commitment organisations, employee-led innovation and sustainable work systems. Attempts to operationalise a unified working definition (European Commission, 2014[4]) have been hindered by this variety of terminology, making it a difficult territory to map and understand. Nevertheless, a common thread across definitions is an emphasis on employee participation and discretionary effort at all levels of the organisation, and full use and development of employees' skills.

By facilitating better utilisation of employees' skills, HPWPs contribute to higher wages and job satisfaction for employees, and higher productivity and lower employee turnover for firms. Based on evidence from

PIAAC, the regular use of at least one type of HPWP within a firm explains a substantial part of the variation in skills use observed across individuals: from 14% of the variation of use of problem solving skills, to 27% in use of reading skills. This makes HPWPs the largest contributor to variance in skills use (more than firm size, skills proficiency, industry, occupation or country effects) (OECD, 2016[3]). At the country level, use of reading and writing skills is strongly related to labour productivity and inclusive economic growth (OECD, 2016[3]). In the context of technological change, jobs that require workers to make frequent use of information-processing skills – literacy, numeracy, and problem solving in technology-rich environments – are also less likely to be automated (Arntz, Gregory and Zierahn, 2016[5]). By improving the way that workers' skills are used in the workplace, HPWPs therefore help to boost employee engagement and firm productivity, while also helping workers to adapt to technological change.

Employees in workplaces that apply HPWP also engage in more learning and demonstrate higher skills than employees in other workplaces. Numerous studies have found that higher levels of training exist in firms with more intensive use of HPWPs (Osterman, 1995[6]; Lynch and Black, 1998[7]; Fialho, Quintini and Vandeweyer, 2019[8]). OECD research finds that in these workplaces, workers are also 12% more likely to engage in informal learning (Fialho, Quintini and Vandeweyer, 2019[8]). Several studies report higher levels of skills among the workforce in organisations with HPWPs (Cappelli and Rogovsky, 1994[9]; Cappelli, 1996[10]; Ashton and Sung, 2002[11]). Not only do workers in such workplaces develop more technical skills, but they also develop the "soft" skills required to work better with others. These are the valuable skills which enable them to communicate effectively and to make problem solving decisions, either on their own or in collaboration with others (Ashton and Sung, 2002[11]).

Box 3.1. Practices that promote better skills use in workplaces

The Australian Workforce and Productivity Agency (formerly Skills Australia) identified the following work organisation practices that make more effective use of skills:

- **Job redesign**: changing the role or description of a job so that the skills of the employee are put to better use. This can include teamwork and flexibility in job descriptions and work arrangements with colleagues.

- **Employee participation**: involving employees in discussions of business strategy, which aims to more effectively use their knowledge and experience.

- **Autonomy**: giving employees more freedom and autonomy to make decisions about how they perform their job.

- **Job rotation**: facilitating the learning of new skills by shifting employees into different jobs and positions within the company.

- **Skills audit** (training needs assessment): aims to identify the skills that employees currently have and identify which skills are most needed.

- **Multi-skilling**: related to job rotation and involves training employees in multiple skill sets, which enables them to perform other tasks not included in their job description.

- **Knowledge transfer**: initiatives to develop new skills and training that is related to work or working with experienced workers to develop mentorship opportunities for younger staff.

Source: Skills Australia (2012[12]), *Better Use of Skills, Better Outcomes: A Research Report on Skills Utilisation in Australia*, Commonwealth of Australia, Canberra, *www.awpa.gov.au/publications/documents/Skills-utilisation-researchreport-15-May-2012.pdf*. Adapted from OECD (2017[13]), *Better Use of Skills in the Workplace: Why it Matters for Productivity and Local Jobs*.

Employees in workplaces with HPWPs also reap greater returns from learning. Fialho, Quintini and Vandeweyer (2019[8]) find that in workplaces with HPWPs, employees enjoy higher returns from formal training, non-formal training, and informal learning. These findings suggest that HPWP may amplify the benefits of learning at work. It could be that workers in HPWP environments receive a different type of training relative to workers in other workplaces. For instance, training may be of higher quality or more closely aligned with employer needs. It could also reflect that workers in HPWP workplaces have more opportunities to translate what they learn from training into immediate use because they have greater flexibility in organising their work. Work organisation practices like job rotation, mentoring, autonomy, task discretion, and teamwork provide opportunities for employees to put newly acquired skills into practice. For instance, coaching or mentoring provides opportunities for a learner to practice a new skill on the job under supervision, which reinforces skill retention and provides the valuable feedback needed for learning. Practices like job rotation (where employees rotate between jobs in the same firm), autonomy, or teamwork provide opportunities to gain experience and new skills by taking on new responsibilities. There is also evidence that training fosters better workplace learning when combined with real development opportunities and a clear career progression roadmap. Martini and Cavanego (2017[14]) find that workers report greater employability gains from career development opportunities like mentoring, job enrichment, job enlargement and job rotation, than from training alone.

High-performance work practices in Canada

In Canada, 28% of firms employ some type of HPWP on a weekly basis (Figure 3.1), which is just ahead of the OECD average (25%), but behind top performers Denmark (41%), Sweden (41%), and New Zealand (34%). The use of HPWP is more common among large firms than in SMEs. Further, high-skilled workers are more likely to be engaged in HPWP than less-skilled workers (OECD, 2019[15]). Certain industries are also more likely to employ HPWPs. Over 35% of firms in information and communications, utilities and professional, scientific and technical services employ HPWP. At the other end of the spectrum, less than 20% of firms in primary industry (agriculture, forestry, fisheries) and transportation and storage do (Figure 3.2). Further, there is variation in the likelihood of employing HPWPs across firms in different provinces and territories. Firms in the central and western provinces of Canada are much more likely to participate in HPWPs on a weekly basis than those in the eastern provinces (Figure 3.3). This likely reflects differences in industry composition across provinces and territories. Box 3.2 shares examples of two Canadian firms employing high-performance work practices.

Figure 3.1. High-performance work practices, Canada and OECD countries, 2012

Share of jobs that employ some type of HPWP on a weekly basis

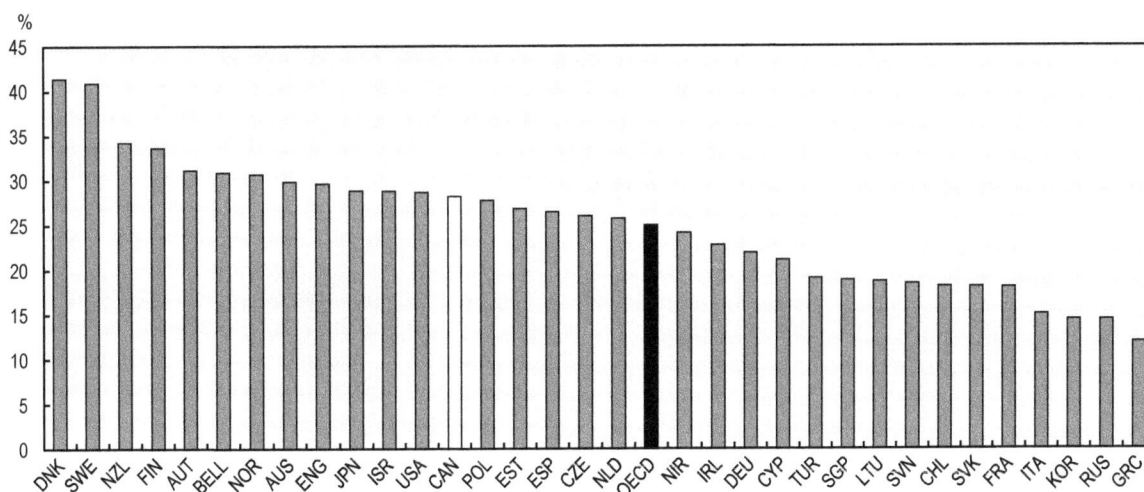

Source: Survey of Adult Skills (PIAAC, 2012, 2015).

Figure 3.2. High-performance work practices by industry, Canada, 2012

Share of jobs that employ some type of HPWP on a weekly basis

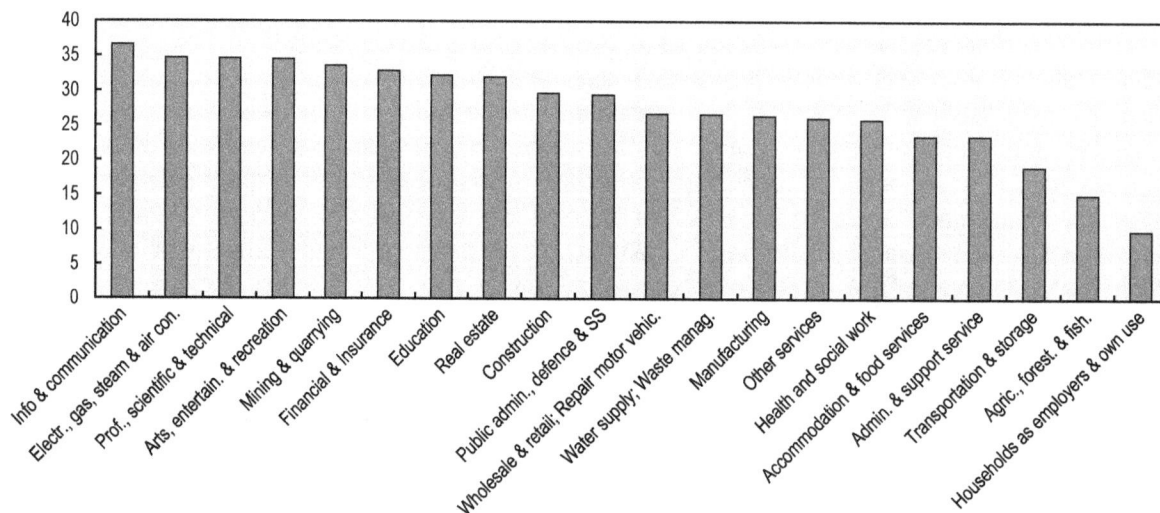

Source: Survey of Adult Skills (PIAAC).

Figure 3.3. High performance work practices by province or territory, Canada, 2012

Share of jobs that employ some type of HPWP on a weekly basis

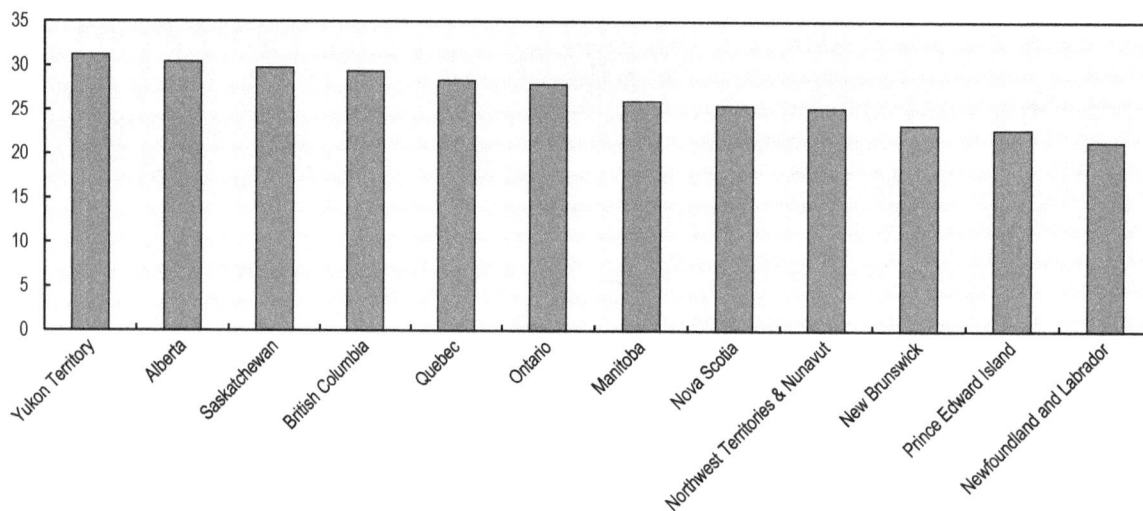

Source: Survey of Adult Skills (PIAAC, 2012, 2015).

Box 3.2. Examples of Canadian firms employing HPWP

Great Place to Work, a certification company, quantifies the current state of a company's workplace culture and shows how it compares to the best organisations. Several top-performing firms employ high-performance work practices like employee involvement in decision-making, mentoring, coaching, and job rotation.

Ceridian has made the Great Place to Work Canada list for organisations with 1 000+ employees consistently over the last five years. Ceridian is an IT/software company based in Toronto, Ontario that employees just over 4 000 employees. The company offers a variety of learning opportunities and experiential initiatives, including a career exploration programme that allows employees to participate in **job rotation** or to job shadow a colleague to see if a job rotation would interest them. New recruits are also paired with a senior leader in the company who acts as a **mentor**.

Habanero ranks #1 on the Great Place to Work Canada list for organisations with fewer than 100 employees. Habanero is an IT consulting firm with 50 employees based in Vancouver, British Columbia. Habanero hosts a monthly meeting (they call it a "Balanced Scorecard Review") to **share information with employees** about last month's performance, why decisions were made and what the resulting outcomes were. Topics include company financials, business development and marketing, clients and new team members. Employees identify Habanero's **coaching** programme as a key driver of high engagement.

Source: https://www.greatplacetowork.ca/en/; www.ceridian.com; www.habaneroconsulting.com.

Barriers to implementing HPWPs in the workplace

Despite the productivity gains and better employee retention experienced by firms that adopt work practices to make better use of employees' skills, relatively few firms employ these practices on a regular basis. As noted above, only 28% of Canadian firms engage in some type of HPWP on a weekly basis. This ranks just above the OECD average (25%).

Lack of awareness of HPWP practices and their benefits

Totterdill et al. (2009[16]) argue that one of the reasons that such practices are not more widespread is the lack of awareness of innovative practices and their benefits among managers, social partners and business support organisations. Employers must be convinced of the benefits of prioritising such practices in order to invest in implementing them.

The costs of poor skills utilisation may be invisible to employers. Change to correct the problem may be seen as risky or costly. Managers may not be aware of their workforce's untapped potential, or else they may not be interested because they rely passively on methods of work organisation and job design that leave little room for skills to be deployed creatively (Keep, 2016[17]). In sectors and businesses that deliver mass services and standardised products, an hierarchical model may deliver profits and work well from the firm's perspective (Ashton and Sung, 2002[11]). Rethinking work organisation and job design under such circumstances is perceived as a risk. On the other hand, in more knowledge-intensive services (e.g. ICT, creative sector, high-end business services and consulting) where the skills and knowledge of the workforce are the core of a competitive product market strategy, the cost of poor skills utilisation is clear and compelling.

There is a misperception among managers that investing in employee training and development increases the risk of poaching by other firms. In fact, firms that invest in training and development have higher employee retention than those that do not (Costen and Salazar, 2011[18]). Workers are more satisfied with their jobs when they have opportunities for training and development. Workers sense that such employers provide good places to work. Investing in training and development is found to have a stronger influence on employee retention if adopted in conjunction with other HPWPs (Kennett, 2013[19]), and if employees are satisfied with the training (Memon, Salleh and Baharom, 2016[20]).

Management skills gap

Implementing HPWPs requires a change in managerial outlook: from supervisor and guardian of knowledge to facilitator and coach (Ashton and Sung, 2002[11]). This can be a difficult transition for many managers to make, one for which they need training. Encouraging flatter hierarchies, more downward flow of information and employee task discretion means that managers derive less authority from their position in the hierarchy. They are now valued for their ability to lead and develop the skills of subordinates. This type of managerial role requires more advanced leadership skills than one based purely on authority. According to the World Management Survey, manufacturing firms in Canada perform above the OECD average in terms of management quality, but fall short of best practice and behind the United States. There is evidence that about 30% of the productivity gap between Canada and the United States can be explained by lower management quality (Bloom, Sadun and Reenen, 2016[21]).

Barriers due to firm size

The likelihood of firms implementing HPWP follows a U shape: HPWPs are most widespread among jobs in large firms and micro (1-10 employees) firms, but are less common in small, mid-size establishments with 11-50 employees (OECD, 2016[3]). SMEs may find it difficult to put in place practices that make the most of their employees' skills because of poor management skills or lack of a specialised HR function (Osterman, 2008[22]). Another difficulty for smaller companies is ensuring there is scope and opportunity for employees to progress and make full use of their skills (Winterbotham et al., 2013[23]). In a small family-owned business, for example, opportunities may not arise until someone retires. This is also the case in micro firms. It may be counterbalanced, however, by the strategy of having employees perform a variety of tasks because the firm is small.

Employee reluctance and the role of unions

HPWPs are associated with greater skills use and as a result, greater job satisfaction and higher wages for employees. This is partly because HPWP requires workers to be more involved in work processes. With that comes the opportunity to develop the social and problem solving skills required for management in addition to the technical skills needed for their immediate work tasks (Ashton and Sung, 2002[11]). HPWPs are clearly seen to benefit employees.

However, employees may be reluctant to adopt new working practices. Interviews with employees in the construction sector in the United Kingdom uncovered reluctance to participate in training or development practices for a variety of reasons. These included concerns about more responsibility, spending time in an office and away from the "tools," or due to a lack of ambition in the sense that they enjoyed their current jobs (Winterbotham et al., 2013[23]). Some negative effects of HPWP have also been noted. For instance, some workers report stress due to the intensification of the work process (Godard and Delaney, 2000[24]). Lowe (2000[25]) provides Canadian examples of instances where HPWPs have been introduced without the adequate involvement of workers in the decision making process; leading employees to experience work changes as negative and stressful rather than positive. This underscores the fundamental importance of engaging openly along the way with workers to build trust and involve them in decisions (Ashton and Sung, 2002[11]).

Unions are concerned when the introduction of new working practices is associated with downsizing and increased employee insecurity (Ashton and Sung, 2002[11]). However, formal agreements can help to build trust by protecting workers' job security and redundancy provisions.

International practice to promote high-performance work practices

The promotion of better skills use within workplaces is still emerging as an area of opportunity for policy. Traditionally, workforce development initiatives have focused on the supply side of labour markets: job search, matching, skills development, and addressing employment barriers faced by vulnerable groups. However, there is increasing recognition of the value of demand-side efforts (OECD/ILO, 2017[13]), including the concept of engaging employers in optimising use of their employees' skills. Several countries have undertaken promising initiatives to promote changes to work organisation, job design and management practices that facilitate better skills use and learning in the workplace, as will be explored below.

Increasingly there has been recognition of the complexity of HPWP, and emphasis on the need to understand how HPWP operates as a system within a particular workplace setting. Determining the threshold level of HPWP implementation that is required for change to be effective was a subject of early work in this field. But recently there has been appreciation that the most effective bundle of practices for a given firm is context-specific (Belt and Giles, 2009[26]). This means that what works for one firm may not work for another. It calls for a comprehensive approach, whereby effects on learning culture and skills use depend on alignment between practices. Indeed one common type of failure observed in practice is "partial change", where the change is not sufficiently systemic and fails to last (Business Decisions Ltd, 2002[27]). For instance, if employees are empowered to apply their skills in creative ways by working in self-managed teams, but lack incentives to keep doing so, the change will likely be temporary. Furthermore, the bundle of new practices should not only be integrated and complimentary, but must also fit with the business strategy of the organisation (Gunderson, 2015[28]). Benefitting from these insights, recent programmes have focused less on implementation of a set of practices, and more on diagnosing the needs of a firm, then experimenting with changes to workplace practices that improve alignment of the whole system.

An important caveat should be underlined. Work organisation, job design and management practices are among the most important factors in influencing skills use within a workplace (OECD, 2016[3]). However, they are not the only factors. Other relevant factors include the innate motivation of employees (Granados and Quintini, forthcoming[29]), various socio-demographic and firm characteristics (Quintini, 2014[30]), as well as institutional and labour market settings, such as employment protection legislation and minimum wage laws (OECD, 2016[3]). These other factors fall outside the scope of the present report.

This section first discusses how different countries conceive of HPWPs. Some view them as a way to improve skills utilisation and productivity, while others focus on outcomes for innovation or job quality. It reviews government approaches that directly address the obstacles discussed above, including supporting experiments to build an evidence base, raising awareness and disseminating best practice, and supporting firms to reshape workplaces. It then discusses different approaches to governance, financing and monitoring of programmes. Finally, it summarizes policy lessons, drawing implications for how Canada could support this type of programme.

Policy focus

Policy efforts to promote HPWP are motivated by a variety of objectives, including skills utilisation, productivity, innovation and job quality (Stone, 2011[31]).

Better skills utilisation is a strong motivation for policy interventions, particularly in countries where the adult population is highly educated and yet productivity growth lags. For example, in **Australia**, where adults are among the most highly educated in the OECD, skills utilisation is recognised as an important element of the country's workforce development strategy (Skills Australia, 2010[32]). The Australian government has made it a priority to increase productivity, employee engagement and satisfaction by making better use of skills in the workplace through strategies that incorporate HPWP. Similarly, **New Zealand** has identified improved utilisation of skills in the workplace as a key focus. The New Zealand government introduced the High Performance Work Initiative in 2011, which supports enterprises in implementing HPWP in order to secure higher productivity.

In other countries, improving quality of working life is the motivation. **Finnish** workplace development programmes target improved working life and productivity. The latest of these programmes, the Liideri programme, established a vision for Finland to have the best working life in Europe by 2020 through improved management and organisation practices. Workplace development agendas in some countries are framed within the context of the digital transformation, understanding that it is likely to have an impact on working life. **Germany's** Ministry of Education and Research (BMBF), for example, launched a Future of Work campaign to promote international cooperation in developing solutions to challenges around the future of work. Topics like flexible hours and lifelong learning are targeted.

Countries sometimes link HPWP programmes to innovation policy. Employees play a key role in successful innovations, by adopting new processes and product technologies (Stone, 2011[31]). The OECD innovation strategy acknowledges that "learning and interaction within organisations and workplaces are at least as important for innovation performance as learning through interactions with external agents. Therefore in order to understand national systems of innovation, it is necessary to bring the organisation of work and employee learning into the analysis" (OECD, 2010[1]). However, many national governments still tend to emphasise technology-based approaches to innovation. Nevertheless, some countries now understand that work organisation matters for innovation. The **Irish** government has made deliberate attempts to integrate its policy for supporting HPWP into its national innovation strategy, emphasising the potential to gain competitive advantage through changes to work organisation.

Government policy can target multiple rationales for supporting HPWP, though policies often highlight one primary objective. This may be due to the compartmentalisation of government structures, where departments concerned with labour and skills issues are distinct from those responsible for innovation. Objectives may also change over time as priorities shift. For instance, **Scotland's** HPWP programme recently gained momentum from new focus on the country's fair work agenda. Previously skills utilisation was a higher priority push in Scotland given its poor productivity record in comparison with England. In a similar way, Finland's workplace development programme (TYKES) was transferred from the Ministry of Labour to Tekes (the Finnish Funding Agency for Innovation, now Business Finland) in 2008. This signalled a shift in policy focus and an attempt to mainstream HPWP programmes as part of the national innovation strategy.

Approaches to encouraging high-performance work practices

Policy initiatives to promote HPWP generally involve one or more of the following activities: supporting applied research, building the evidence base, raising awareness, disseminating good practice, and funding workplace interventions. These activities complement one other. Expertise built during research activities informs workplace interventions, and case studies resulting from funded projects demonstrate the benefits of HPWP to the wider population. Governments taking a "soft" interventionist approach might simply raise awareness by disseminating good practice. Governments taking a "harder" interventionist approach could support applied research and workplace interventions.

Supporting research and building the evidence base

Research-oriented programmes generate an evidence base about which types of practices are most effective at building learning organisations. Several countries support research to develop the evidence base around workplace innovation. For example, in **Australia**, the Centre for Workplace Leadership was established in 2013 as a joint initiative between the Australian Federal Government Department of Employment and the University of Melbourne's Faculty of Businesses and Economics. Its research focuses on building the capability of frontline leadership, creating and sustaining a HPWP culture, and transforming workplaces through technology and workplace innovation. In **Sweden**, the government agency for innovation, Vinnova, has invested in research programmes on workplace innovation and innovation management. Vinnova's Working Life initiatives aim to strengthen innovation capacity in industry and the public sector by improving organisational conditions for competitiveness and growth (Döös and Wilhelmson, 2009[33]).

Raising awareness and disseminating best practices

As noted above, many employers are simply not aware of the value of implementing HPWPs. Findings from a review of English SMEs showed that one of the most effective methods to persuade firms to adopt HPWP is to share concrete evidence from the experiences of similar firms (Stone et al., 2012[34]). Such first-hand evidence clarifies what adoption of HPWP could mean in their workplace.

Online databases and learning platforms can help to display the benefits of HPWP. For example, the European Workplace Innovation Network (EUWIN**)** is a **Europe**-wide network launched in 2013 by the European commission and Workplace Innovation Europe. It disseminates evidence of the benefits of workplace innovation via online tools and platforms, regional workshops and social media. Similarly, the HiPAir project, co-funded by the Erasmus+ programme of the European Commission, shares case studies of exemplary aviation companies that have successfully implemented HPWPs via the HPWP Collaboration Platform (www.hpwp.eu). Both EUWIN and the HiPAir project produce online learning resources (e.g. how-to guides, training curricula, and tools) to support employers interested in implementing HPWP in their workplaces. Such tools spur other employers to proceed.

Diagnostic tools and self-assessment surveys provide an affordable way for firms to assess their current work organisation and management practices. The Workplace Innovation Toolkit in **Ireland** is an online questionnaire that facilitates a business in self-evaluation of their capacity to become a more innovative workplace. It focuses on employee engagement, innovation, productivity and training. The toolkit encourages businesses to be proactive in transforming their work practices by quickly identifying areas for improvement. It then guides users to relevant supports. Similarly, the Workplace Innovation Diagnostic Survey developed by Workplace Innovation Europe (WIE) is an online employee survey tool that helps employers identify areas for improvement in enhancing employee engagement and performance (Box 3.3). It focuses on workplace practices that enable people at every level to use their full range of skills, knowledge, experience and creativity. Online talent management tools are also being used by firms for employee career development. The tools suggest opportunities for job rotation, training, or mentorship within the firm based on the employee's inputted skills, interests and experience. A global survey of HR professionals suggests that 6% of firms are using talent management tools (Oracle, 2019[35]).

Conferences and seminars can be a cost-effective way to share best practices with a large group of employers at the same time. **Scotland's** national economic development agency, Scottish Enterprise, offers master classes in workplace innovation targeted at leaders of growing businesses who are dealing with issues relating to leadership, staff engagement and culture. These workshops are delivered by practitioners from WIE with organisational change expertise. Following the master class, business leaders can continue with peer learning and ongoing support through the WIE online platform.

Box 3.3. Workplace Innovation Diagnostic Survey

The Workplace Innovation Diagnostic is an employee survey tool created by Workplace Innovation Europe. It is designed to pinpoint areas for improvement within firms, using 62 evidence-based indicators that are strongly associated with high performance and employee well-being. The survey aims to help companies improve employee engagement, foster a positive workplace culture and improve business productivity and performance.

The survey asks employees and managers to rate on a scale from one (strongly disagree) to ten (strongly agree) their agreement with statements related to four elements of workplace practice:

- Job design, teams and technology (E.g. "Team members meet as a group to plan their own work and to discuss ways of improving how they do it.")

- Organisational structures, management and procedures (E.g. "Decision-making is delegated to the lowest practical level; managers do not micro-manage those below them.")

- Employee-driven improvement and Innovation (E.g. "Employees enjoy abundant opportunities to identify improvements in their own areas of work.")

- Co-created leadership and employee voice (E.g. "The organisation believes in an open approach to sharing strategic information with employees.")

After employees and managers complete the survey, experts at WIE translate the diagnostic results into an action plan. According to WIE, organisations that systematically adopt evidence-based workplace practices see a 20-60 per cent improvement across a range of indicators, including productivity, employee health and well-being (Workplace Innovation Europe, 2019b[36]).

Source: Workplace Innovation Europe (2019a[37]), *The Workplace Innovation Diagnostic*, http://www.workplaceinnovation.eu/LWIP-The-Workplace-Innovation-Diagnostic; Workplace Innovation Europe (2019b[36]), *Workplace Innovation Europe*, https://workplaceinnovation.eu/.

National standards for best human resource development practices provide an incentive for employers to upgrade (Ashton and Sung, 2002[11]). Some governments offer national awards for employers who meet the standards, as with the Malcolm Baldridge Awards in the United States and the Investors in People (IiP) programme in the United Kingdom. To achieve these awards, organisations must demonstrate to independent assessors that their HR practices meet national standards. The Malcolm Baldridge Awards emphasise employment practices like careful selection, training, and performance evaluation while the IiP programme emphasises effective communication, evaluation of performance and a systematic approach to training. Neither standard is explicitly modelled on HPWP. Nevertheless, it typically takes UK organisations almost two years to reach the standard, suggesting that the process of change can be an important learning exercise. Survey evidence also suggests that the achievement of IiP status in the United Kingdom is associated with higher levels of skills among the workforce in these companies, especially in terms of newly developed soft skills. Appelbaum and Batt (1994[38]) argue that the Baldrige awards influence the work organisation and management practices of firms beyond those that receive awards. The awards encourage networking and benchmarking among other firms who contact winners for advice.

Social actors play a key role in raising awareness of HPWP and presenting HPWP as a win-win for employers and workers. The role of social actors is elaborated later in this chapter.

Workplace interventions

Simply raising awareness and elucidating the business case for HPWP may not be enough. Employers may still be sceptical. General "sales pitches" are less effective than case studies that highlight benefits for a particular sector or size of firm. In that spirit, some governments subsidise workplace interventions. Generally such support takes the form of staff or management training, hiring external experts to support management in upgrading workplace organisation. Interventions can target individual firms, but increasingly countries are choosing to direct support at networks of firms to capture learning and cost-efficiency advantages.

It is unrealistic to expect government to help all firms improve their work organisation and job design, Support is often directed at a limited number of businesses which are then used as role models (OECD, 2016[3]). For example, the Best Practice Demonstration Program (BPDP) in **Australia,** established by the federal government in 1991, aimed to develop 'best practice firms' to serve as demonstrations to other organisations of ways to implement new approaches to working (Healy, 2003[39]). Financial support was given to firms willing to adopt best practice principles. Forty-three medium and large enterprises were selected from diverse industry sectors and regions. One of the criterion for selection was previous good relations with labour groups. The programme included a media campaign of successful case studies as well as a requirement that firms network with non-funded firms. The impact on non-funded firms was not, however, evaluated (Stone, 2011[31]).

An advantage of directing interventions at individual firms is the possibility to provide tailored support. For example, in **New Zealand,** firms can apply for co-funding from the national innovation agency (Callaghan Innovation) to participate in a coaching programme. The programme is designed to improve work practices, build an innovation culture and increase employee engagement by matching firms with external specialist consultants. Similarly, the Partners at Work Grants Programme, launched in 2002 by the government in **Victoria, Australia**, offers competitive grants to fund consultancy services to support workplace change and training programmes. An evaluation conducted in 2006 among participating firms revealed that the programme resulted in improved communication and trust between management and staff, more effective management practices and the creation of a culture of participation (Stone, 2011[31]). In **North-Rhine Westphalia Germany**, the state-owned Innovative Employment Promotion Company (GIB) supports 1500 companies annually to collaborate with expert organisations in workplace innovation and modernisation (Oeij, Rus and Pot, 2017[40]). It supports both short-term workplace change projects in SMEs, as well as longer-term projects that involve development of management strategy. A disadvantage of directing workplace innovation initiatives at individual employers, however, is that the resulting programmes can be too firm specific. They may fail to resolve broader sectoral or national skills challenges (OECD/ILO, 2017[13]).

Countries are increasingly directing policy interventions at networks, rather than at individual firms. Encouraging multiple actors to organise and coordinate with each other to address workplace challenges can be an effective way to implement HPWP. Network-focused initiatives encourage firms to maintain HPWP initiatives after funding ends and facilitates the transfer of knowledge between firms (Stone, 2011[41]). Strengthened partnerships and coordination amongst businesses promotes peer learning, which can sustain longer-term impacts. A peer learning approach may also be effective at raising awareness among employers about the benefits of HPWP, as employers may more readily accept advice from other employers rather than from public actors. Sharing consulting services across multiple firms is also cost-effective.

A number of such network-focused programmes exist. In **Finland**, TYKES used to fund learning network projects. These were joint learning forums consisting of researchers and businesses. External experts facilitated the coordination. These learning networks aimed to increase the developmental expertise of the participants, create and experiment with new forms of development cooperation between R&D institutions and workplaces, and generate innovative solutions for Finnish working life (Alasoini, 2019[42]). **Scottish Enterprise** worked with Workplace Innovation Europe's Fresh Thinking Labs to develop its programme model, which recruits a network of ten firms and equips them with expert consultants who guide them through a process of workplace change from diagnosis to implementation (Box 3.4). Firms are selected through referrals from Scottish Enterprise's account managers who have developed relationships with over

2 000 companies. The selected firms come from a diverse range of sectors and participate in a peer support network where they can share and collectively overcome challenges faced in HPWP implementation. In the **French** Anact model, fifty firms are involved in the learning network, ten receive intensive consulting support, while the other forty firms learn from the experiences of the participant firms.

Box 3.4. Scottish Enterprise

Workplace innovation is a key policy focus of the Scottish government's inclusive growth strategy and fair work framework. Scottish Enterprise, the national economic development agency, launched an awareness-raising campaign that included workshops, master classes and support services to increase the adoption of workplace innovation practices. They also hired Workplace Innovation Europe to deliver the Workplace Innovation Engagement Programme (WIEP).

Companies in the WIEP participate in a workplace diagnostic survey, followed by eight structured learning workshops, five action-learning sessions, and 14 hours of individual in-company coaching or facilitation. The recruitment and selection of companies for the programme depends on referrals by Scottish Enterprise's account managers who work with senior management teams in over 2 000 companies to identify their business needs and potential. They shortlist potential companies suitable for the programme. Account managers pay special attention to firms in which senior management are committed to making changes based on the diagnostic results. Ten companies were recruited for the first cohort of the programme in 2016 and nine more companies were recruited in 2017.

An evaluation of the programme showed that where companies implemented HPWP, qualitative benefits included improved efficiency, enhanced collaboration between teams, better problem solving and greater employee empowerment. The creation of peer-to-peer learning networks among the participant firms was effective in providing peer support and encouragement for participating companies, especially in empowering participants to overcome resistance to workplace innovation within their companies. This approach was viewed to be a powerful and cost-effective means of supporting the wider adoption of HPWP in Scotland.

Source: Exton, R. and P. Totterdill (2019[43]) , "Unleashing workplace innovation in Scotland", International Journal of Technology Transfer and Commercialisation, https://doi.org/10.1504/ijttc.2019.10021356.

Participants in a learning network generally have a common interest, and may be from the same region, sector, value chain, or the same position in a value chain. Working with networks of firms from the same sector can be a particularly effective model, as it takes advantage of existing employer networks and supply chains. Supporting firms to implement workplace innovation requires a deep level of expertise about a firm's activities and work organisation needs, which can be sector-specific. For example, during one of the **Scottish** Funding Council's pilot projects, staff supervisors in care homes provided advice to management about how to redesign the jobs of staff in the health care sector. Staff had complained that their jobs had not changed after training. Sector-based approaches may hold up individual employers within the sector as role models, or position larger employers to play a lead role in catalysing change within their supply chains. **Korea**'s Training Consortium for SMEs provides a good example of this latter approach. The consortium facilitates joint training between large companies and SMEs in their supply chain. The large company provides customised training to reinforce the human resource management capability of the SMEs in their supply chain.

Evidence is mixed as to whether network-focused programmes lead to widespread dissemination and learning. The partnership model was judged to be a strength of the Workplace Skills Initiative (WSI) in **Canada**. WSI was introduced by Human Resources and Skills Development Canada (currently known as Employment and Social Development Canada) in 2005 to stimulate partnership-based projects. The projects either tested innovative approaches to workplace skills development or supported the adoption of improved human resources management practices and sharing of best practices. An 2012 evaluation report found that the partnership approach increased collaboration and contributed to increased knowledge of human resources management and workplace skills development. The most significant challenge was a lack of sustained adoption over time of practices among recipient and partner organisations. This was primarily due to financial barriers (HRSDC, 2012[44]). Projects also tended to be focused on skills development rather than on improvements to human resources management. Qualitative evaluations of the Finnish TYKE and TYKES programmes (Box 3.5) found they were effective in promoting workplace innovation and productivity, but that they did not achieve the widespread dissemination and learning benefits that had been hoped for (Arnkil, 2004[45]; Oosi et al., 2010[46]).

Box 3.5. Finnish workplace innovation programmes

Finland has been a leader in workplace innovation since its first workplace development programme in the mid-1990s. The Ministry of Labour launched the Finnish Workplace Development Programme (TYKE) in 1996, and replaced it with the TYKES programme in 2004. Both programmes were created to develop productivity and the quality of working life in Finland. In 2008, responsibility for the TYKES programme was transferred from the Ministry of Labour to Tekes (the Finnish Funding Agency for Technology and Innovation, now Business Finland). This transfer was part of the adoption of a new national innovation strategy that emphasises demand-driven and non-technological innovation. The latest of these national workplace innovation programmes is the Liideri Business, Productivity and Joy at Work Programme. It aims to promote management and organisational practices that improve business activities and working life.

The TYKES programme was based on the view that the most effective way to generate innovative solutions is through learning and cooperation between workplaces, research and development units and policy makers (Alasoini, 2019[42]). TYKES therefore focused on funding learning network projects, which convened firms and researchers to work together in learning forums.

While the Liideri Programme also aimed to enhance the cooperation between researchers and firms, it placed a stronger emphasis on action-oriented research. The programme funded research projects to understand the impacts of employee-involved innovation, new forms of work organisation and management practices. Companies, universities, research institutes, and polytechnics were invited to apply for funding to develop expertise in these areas. Funding action-oriented research also helps to build a pool of experts in workplace innovation. This is seen as crucial to providing expert support to businesses.

Source: Alasoini, T. (2019[42]), "The Promotion of Workplace Innovation in Finland", *Finnish Institute of Occupational Health.*

Given public funding constraints, policy initiatives are often targeted to where there is the most potential for uptake or the most need for change. In Finland, government officials decided to limit programme support to export-oriented and growth-oriented firms. However, this approach excluded many SMEs. As noted above, SMEs are less likely to implement HPWPs than larger firms. A firm's ability to benefit from HPWPs depends on the capacity of its managers (OECD, 2016[3]). Better management quality can boost the creativity and innovation potential of workers (Alasoni, 2019). For this reason, some initiatives, like the Finnish Liideri Programme and the former Canada Workplace Skills Initiative, specifically reach out to SMEs. In other countries, only SMEs are eligible for participation. For example, the **Korean** Subsidies for Learning Organisations build the capacity of SMEs specifically by offering a series of subsidies. The first set of subsidies are to hire external consultants to analyse the company's training needs, to develop capacity-building training for higher and senior management staff, and to provide guidance programmes to help companies become organisations that foster learning and development. The second set of subsidies are available for companies to create and manage learning groups, and to provide training to higher management responsible for the learning activities. The final set of subsidies allows companies to take part in peer-learning activities and to share their experience in building a learning organisation. Korea's experience highlights the importance of complementing HPWP initiatives with management skills development programmes, as low management skills can be a bottleneck to workplace innovation.

Workplace innovation programmes to increase business productivity are traditionally targeted at the private sector (Eurofound, 2016[47]), though this is starting to change. Fostering innovative workplace organisation practices in the public sector may be viewed as new and risky, running contrary to the perceived role of bureaucratic organisations to deliver consistent public services (OECD, 2017[48]). However, the number of workplace innovation programmes in the public sector is growing. In Europe, WIE organises workshops specifically for the public sector on how to implement workplace innovation practices for improved skills use and performance. The Government of Canada has recently piloted a digital platform that enables selection of public servants for inter-departmental projects based on their skills and behaviours rather than their education credentials. This initiative helps to make better use of employees' skills and supports employee retention in the public service (Box 3.6). Learning how the private sector fosters workplace innovation can be instructive for the public sector. In New South Wales in Australia, the regional government encourages the public sector to consult with firms in the not-for-profit and private sectors about implementing innovative changes to workplace organisation (PSE, 2013[49]).

Box 3.6. Workplace innovation in the public sector

Piloting the Government of Canada's Free Agent model

The Canadian government has been testing models for recruiting and mobilising talent in the public service in the digital age. Free Agents is a pilot digital platform for human resources that features a competency validation process and easy search functions. The objectives of the pilot were to support, develop and retrain talented public servants and to increase the capacity of the public service to innovate and solve problems. Free Agents represents a departure from the permanent hiring model in the Canadian public service, which is cost and time intensive. The new model enables organisation of talent and skills for inter-departmental project-based work rather than the traditional public sector model of working within department silos and hierarchies. As part of the pilot, candidates ("free agents") who demonstrated core attributes were offered lateral deployments. The programme staffed 42 projects in 20 departments during the first year. The majority of participants reported new opportunities to apply existing skills and develop new skills, and a higher likelihood of remaining in the public service.

Source: OECD (2018[50]), "Case Study: Free agents and GC talent cloud – Canada", https://www.oecd.org/gov/innovative-government/Canada-case-study-UAE-report-2018.pdf.

Governance and Financing

This section explores models of governance and financing for programmes supporting high-performance work practices.

Link to workforce development

In some countries, including the United Kingdom and Australia, workplace innovation programmes (or skills utilisation or HPWP programmes) are part of a larger workforce development strategy.

The **UK** Commission for Employment and Skills managed workforce innovation programmes (e.g. the Employer Ownership for Skills, UK Futures programme) as well as a skills utilisation project. The latter consisted of a literature review on skills utilisation, the development of an employer survey tool to assess take-up of HPWP, a series of case studies to understand how HPWP is implemented in real-life workplaces, and a policy review to establish what policies were already being deployed to encourage wider take-up.

In **Australia**, skills utilisation is recognised as an important element of the country's workforce development strategy (Skills Australia, 2010[32]). The Australian Workforce and Productivity Agency (AWPA) was an independent statutory body, under the Department of Industry since 2014, responsible for providing advice to the government on current and future skills and workforce development needs. It managed the National Workforce Development Fund, which provided funding of AUD 700 million over 5 years to partnerships between registered training organisations and firms or groups of firms to carry out skills development initiatives. It also managed a skills utilisation project that included a literature review, a publication of case studies, and a research report on the organisational dynamics need within firms for skills utilisation programmes to succeed (Skills Australia, 2012[12]).

Centralised versus decentralised leadership

Coordination between federal, state and local bodies is managed differently across countries. Countries that manage and finance HPWP programmes at the national level embed such programmes in wider policy and department structures. This approach has the advantage of alignment with national strategic goals. For example, in **Finland**, workplace innovation is incorporated in the National Innovation Strategy. Business Finland directs public financing to projects aimed at HPWP research and implementation. Legislation and a long tradition of social partnership has facilitated the inclusion of HPWP in the national agenda. The Finnish model of "high union density, centralised bargaining, tripartite machinery and consultation structures and procedures" (Stone and Braidford, 2008[51]) underlies the establishment of workplace innovation as a permanent research focus in Business Finland (Totterdill et al., 2009[16]).

Similarly, in **Ireland** workplace innovation is integrated into the country's wider national policy framework as part of the National Workplace Strategy (NWS). The NWS, adopted in 2005, aims to stimulate workplace change and innovation by recognising the role that workplace partnership can play in this process. The High Level Implementation Group (HLIG), under the authority of the Department of Enterprise, Trade and Employment, is responsible for the implementation of the NWS. HLIG membership includes senior government representatives across ministries, trade unions and employer associations. In addressing the comprehensive agenda set out in the NWS, the HLIG is viewed as "a unique and effective forum for government and social partners to initiate and monitor approaches to supporting workplace development in an innovative and joined-up manner" (NCCP, 2007[52]).

New Zealand provides another example of a national governance model supported by working groups. The New Zealand government launched the Workplace Productivity Agenda in 2005 with a goal of positioning workplace productivity issues within the wider policy agenda. It also established the Workplace Productivity Reference Group consisting of representatives from unions and employer groups. The purpose of the working group is to advise government on workplace productivity issues and to help implement its HPWP strategy. Joint responsibility for action among industry, firms, unions, employees and government is a key component of the national agenda.

Nationally-governed programmes enjoy greater political momentum and alignment with national strategic goals. However, this may come at a cost. The programmes may be less tailored to the regional or sectoral context. Decentralised governance of HPWP programmes may foster stronger relationships with social partners, a key component of successful HPWP implementation. For example in **North Rhine-Westphalia (NRW)** in **Germany,** the GIB (Innovative Employment Promotion Company) – a federal state consultant organisation for NRW – launched the Work-Oriented Modernisation Programme that finances the development of workplaces through collaborations between experts and industries. The programme aims to increase the competitiveness of SMEs and modernise work organisation, lifelong learning and employability. The programme focuses on providing consultancy and disseminating innovative workplace practices. In Australia, the state of **Victoria** has also been a leader in actively promoting HPWP. Business

Victoria, a branch of the State of Victoria's Department of Business and Innovation, was set up to support businesses to implement HPWP. Most of their activities focus on raising awareness about HPWP among firms, including the creation of a High Performance Toolkit that includes factsheets on topics like workplace change, flexibility and organisational diversity.

A promising governance model employed in several countries involves national-level leadership combined with sub-national implementation. **France's** Anact provides a good example. It is governed and financed at the national level, but implemented by regional bodies (Box 3.7). Another example is the Innovative Workplaces case study in the **United Kingdom**. This was a collaboration between a national public body (Acas), a regional development agency (EMDA), and an NGO (UKWON). Eleven companies were recruited to participate in the programme, which consisted of courses and meetings to develop HPWP action plans. Independent evaluations showed that the programme was successful in generating a 4:1 return on public investments, as well as other less tangible benefits such as increased levels of employee engagement, morale and trust (OECD/ILO, 2017[13]).

Box 3.7. France's Anact

The National Bureau for the Improvement of Working Conditions (*L'Agence Nationale pour l'Amélioration des Conditions de Travail,* Anact) was set up in 1973 against a backdrop of industrial relations conflict (Totterdill et al., 2009[16]). Anact was created as a national agency, involving social partners but funded by the state. While initially focused on helping firms to improve working conditions, the agency's portfolio has evolved to include improving quality of working life and social dialogue, promoting gender equality in the workplace and supporting organisation and managerial innovation.

Anact supports companies to innovate their workplaces through the Fund for the Improvement of Working Conditions (*Le Fonds pour l'amélioration des conditions de travail,* FACT). In 2017, FACT put out a call for proposals for firms to implement new forms of work organisation and management practices. Some 27 projects were selected with an overall budget of EUR 753 000. One third of the selected projects were territorial, sectoral and collective action projects, and the remainder were individual firms or associations.

As a national agency, Anact works closely with 16 regional associations for the improvement of working conditions (Aract). Each Aract addresses nationally defined priorities relating to working life and productivity. Yet they function in a way that is locally negotiated. The Anact-Aract network supports SMEs and other organisations in improving working conditions beyond the regulatory minimum. Supports include sharing tested tools and methods, diagnostic support, and collective action programmes to mobilise networks of small companies to implement workplace innovation (Anact, 2019[53]).

The national government allocates the budget and sets the operational priorities for both the Anact and Aracts. This ensures that the whole country is working towards the same goals. But while there is a formal planning agreement with each of the regions reflecting nationally defined priorities, these are broad and allow for regional tailoring.

Source: Anact (2019[53]), *Services et outils du réseau Anact-Aract,* https://www.anact.fr/les-services-et-outils-proposes-par-le-reseau-anact-aract; Totterdill, P. et al. (2009[16]), *Workplace Innovation in European Countries,* Report to KOWIN. UK Work Organisation Network, Nottingham.

Role of social partners

A central feature of successful programmes promoting HPWP is the commitment of social partners. Working together with employers and unions to promote HPWP helps governments overcome resistance by presenting the change as a win-win option for both employers and workers. Engaging social partners in HPWP is seen as an essential part of building a broad coalition of support, which helps to sustain programme duration. Successful programmes are often coordinated within a social partnership framework, usually government, employers and unions, and sometimes research institutes. But even in countries where social partnership arrangements are not as developed, effort is still made to draw social partners into the policy process.

Notably, the involvement of social partners in workplace innovation is mandated by legislation in some countries. The **German** co-determination model requires that employees participate in workplace or enterprise decision-making. In practice, workers' participation is indirect in that it operates through employee representatives and formalised co-determination bodies. Similarly, in **Sweden**, 'Medbestämmandelagen' or co-determination laws promote employee participation in decision-making on employment and working conditions. These co-determination laws require employers to negotiate with unions before making major changes to business strategy or practice (OECD, 2016[3]).

In countries where social partnership is not legislated, there is still collaboration between employers and unions in promoting HPWP. For example in **Denmark**, the Danish Confederation of Trade Unions' (LO) plays a large role in promoting employee-driven innovation in private and public sector workplaces. The LO compiled a report and pamphlet of best workplace practices that support employee-driven innovation as a source of inspiration for Danish companies and political decision makers (LO, 2007[54]). The Danish government also concluded a tripartite agreement on adult and continuing training for the period 2018 to 2021, together with LO, and the Confederation of Danish Employers. The agreement includes the creation of funds for employees to undertake training on their own, awareness raising activities, courses to improve basic literacy and numeracy skills, skill recognition and improved training guidance. In **Australia**, the Best Practice Demonstration Programme was organised through a tripartite structure established by the Australian federal government in 1991. **New Zealand** developed specific tripartite arrangements to support HPW, including the Workplace Productivity Agenda and the Workplace Productivity Reference Group. Social partners oversee the implementation of the Department of Labour's Workplace Productivity Agenda.

In the **United Kingdom**, Unionlearn is the learning and skills organisation of the Trades Union Congress. It supports workers in acquiring skills and qualifications to improve their employability. One of its key activities is the training of Union Learning Representatives (ULRs), who help workers identify their training needs, then arrange learning opportunities within their companies. Since its inception, Unionlearn has trained more than 40 000 URLs and over a quarter of a million people benefit from training and learning opportunities. At an individual level, ULRs help employees progress at work, finding opportunities for meaningful work that uses their skills and knowledge. A Unionlearn research report found that in firms where industrial relations are good, union officials exercise greater influence over practices such as job design, progression and redeployment (Jameson, 2012[55]).

In the **United States**, UpSkill America is an employer-led movement that promotes training and advancement practices. The association developed a step-by-step training tool to encourage employers to create upskilling programmes that focus on soft skills. The tool recommends practices like job rotation and peer-to-peer coaching.

Financial cost of programmes

It can be difficult to gauge the precise financial cost of programmes to promote HPWP, since they are often bundled together with wider workforce development support.

Spending on national HPWP programmes tends to be modest, especially when programmes are less intensive, e.g. focused on building awareness or targeting a small number of companies. One review estimates that most HPWP programmes amount to less than EUR 1 per capita on average (Stone, 2011[31]). **Finland** stood out in this review as spending the most on programmes (the TYKES Workplace Development Programme budget was EUR 15 million per year or EUR 3.5 per capita). Table 3.1 summarises the cost of workplace interventions across countries (Table 3.1).

Some programmes cover the cost of carrying out an evaluation. For example, the TYKES programme in **Finland** engaged an external evaluator with a budget of EUR 120 000 to conduct interviews with participants of workplace development projects (Alasoini, 2019[42]). An independent evaluation was also a requirement for the Innovative Workplaces Programme in the **United Kingdom**. An estimated 20 per cent (GBP 48 000) of project funding was allocated to evaluation costs (Harris et al., 2011[56]).

Table 3.1. Examples of average funding for workplace innovation grants

	Workplace innovation programme	Total programme funding	Average funding per grant	Duration of programme
Finland	TYKES Workplace Development Programme	EUR 75 million	EUR 320 000	2004-2010
Finland	Liideri Joy at Work Programme	EUR 67 million	EUR 209 000	2012-2018
Australia	Best Practice Demonstration Program	AUD 18 million	AUD 418 600	1991-1994
East Midlands, United Kingdom	Innovative Workplaces Programme	GBP 236 000	GBP 23 600	2009-2010
France	FACT fund to support organisation and managerial innovation	EUR 754 000	EUR 28 000	2017
Ireland	Workplace Innovation Fund	EUR 9 million	EUR 273 000	2007-2009

Source: Alasoini, T. (2019[42]), "The Promotion of Workplace Innovation in Finland", Finnish Institute of Occupational Health; Anact (2017[57]), *Appel à projets "Innovations organisationnelles et managériales"*; Harris, L. et al., (2011[56]), *A Review of the 'Innovative Workplaces' Initiative* Totterdill, P. et al. (2009[16]), Workplace Innovation in European Countries, Report to KOWIN. UK Work Organisation Network, Nottingham.

Monitoring and evaluation of programmes

Relative to supply-side skills development policies, programmes to promote skills utilisation and HPWP are more difficult to evaluate because they lack clear and direct metrics (Keep, 2016[17]). Nevertheless, Keep (2016[17]) suggests some indicators that might be used in the context of firm or sector-level HPWP interventions: productivity increases, cost savings, increased sales, quality improvements, reported levels of innovation, reduced employer and employee perceptions of skills mismatches, reduced staff turnover, and enhanced employee satisfaction. However, firms may not have the information and monitoring systems to gather this data on a routine basis.

A handful of efforts to evaluate HPWP programmes use both quantitative and qualitative methods. The evaluation of the Innovative Workplaces programme in East Midlands in **England** is an example of this mixed-method approach. The independent evaluation encompassed qualitative interviews with programme participants, as well as a quantitative analysis of the costs and benefits to participating organisations. The economic impact assessment reported an overall minimum return on investment of GBP 4 for every GBP 1 of public sector expenditure (OECD/ILO, 2017[13]). The **EU** HipAir Project does not use independent evaluators, but instead guides participating firms in the use of a Return on Investment (ROI) calculator. After inputting estimated costs and benefits from an HPWP implementation, employers obtain an estimated ROI from the online calculator.

Most efforts to evaluate workplace innovation programmes have been qualitative rather than quantitative in nature. This is not surprising given the challenges described above. Qualitative surveys and self-assessments are common evaluation methods for these types of programmes. For example, to evaluate the TYKE programme in **Finland**, representatives from management, personnel, and external experts submitted self-assessments after the project ended. The survey included 15 questions on operational performance, quality of working life and equality in the workplace (Alasoini, 2019[42]). **Scotland** applied a qualitative case study approach to evaluate its skill utilisation pilot projects. Questions were asked of participants before, during and after project completion to understand what worked, what did not work and why, and how participants rated their experiences of the project (Keep, 2016[17]). Similarly, in the WIEP in Scotland, participating firms completed the same diagnostic survey at the start and end of the project to assess the impact of the workplace transformation.

There are limitations in the capacity of monitoring and evaluation exercises to measure the full impact of programmes to stimulate and promote HPWP. Most evaluations only capture short-term impacts. But benefits arising from introducing HPWPs often require several years to materialise (Stone, 2011[31]). Available funding for evaluation typically ends shortly after programme implementation, hampering valuable longer-term follow-up.

Little is known about whether interventions have benefits for firms that do not directly participate in the programme. Diffusion effects are difficult to measure. An OECD (forthcoming[58]) report on responding to the future of work recommends re-visiting a comprehensive and regular employer survey in Canada, building on the previous Workplace and Employee Survey. A regular enterprise survey that tracks work organisation, job design, management and training practices as well as information about skills gaps can be useful for monitoring national progress on HPWP adoption and skills utilisation. Both Australia and the United Kingdom conduct regular national-level enterprise surveys.

Policy lessons

Several useful policy lessons can be drawn from reviews of international programmes to support HPWP (Eurofound, 2015[59]; Stone, 2011[31]; Totterdill et al., 2009[16]):

- For HPWP uptake to be effective, programmes should be adapted to individual workplaces. Since effective HPWP implementation requires managers to be coaches and facilitators, investing in management skills may be a necessary first step.

- Financial support is often provided to hire experts who assist firms to develop and implement firm-specific solutions in workplace innovation. Doing so requires a pool of experts that can be developed over time. Investment in applied research helps to build understanding of the concepts and frameworks involved.

- For impacts to be long lasting and widespread, policymakers must build and sustain a broad coalition of support for workplace innovation programmes. Otherwise, as was observed with some national level programmes in Europe, a change in political power can be sufficient to end the programme. Social partners should be involved to build awareness of the importance of HPWP. Sustainable policy engagement with HPWP programmes calls for actions with a long time horizon, coupled with strong frameworks and infrastructure in place to sustain them.

- Use of collaborative learning networks can be a cost effective way to raise awareness and implement workplace innovation initiatives. Learning networks encourage firms to share knowledge and benefit from peer support. Governments can share the experiences of role models, offer networking sessions and master classes, and establish HR benchmarks. Diagnostic tools provide a good starting point for firms to assess their current work organisation and management practices and to obtain suggestions about steps they could take to design and implement better practices.

- Programmes governed at the national level benefit from political momentum and better alignment with national strategic goals. Decentralised programmes respond better to local contexts. In some countries, programmes benefit from national level leadership while regional bodies manage implementation. This cooperation framework allows regional actors to design an approach that is specific to the region's needs while being aligned to a broader national skills and innovation agenda.

Assessment and recommendations

Evidence strongly suggests that high-performance work practices contribute to better skills use and foster workplaces that support informal learning. Such practices are not widespread in Canada, however, and little policy attention has been focused on expanding their use. Workforce development initiatives traditionally focus on the supply side of labour markets, e.g. improving the matching of job seekers with jobs, retraining workers in higher-demand sectors, and helping job seekers to overcome barriers to employment and education and training. Canadian provinces could consider expanding their workforce development and innovation programmes to prioritise improved skills use and developing learning organisations within workplaces. Recognising skills utilisation as an important element of Canada's workforce development strategy, as Australia and the United Kingdom have done, would support Canada's productivity and innovation agenda. It would also help adults to adapt to the changing demand for skills.

Provincial **workforce innovation centers** could allocate a portion of their research funding to testing and evaluating approaches to better skills utilisation within workplaces. This would fall within their existing mandate to "support the research, testing and sharing of ideas and models of innovation in workforce development". The governance structure of WICs is already well set up to support such a workplace innovation programme. Based on the NLWIC case study, stakeholder engagement ranks as a core activity of the WICs. They have succeeded in building strong networks that include employers, employer groups, trade unions, employment service providers, and training institutions. WICs also have experience administering research funding. Furthermore, they are starting to build the evaluation and monitoring capacity of participants. However, failing an increase in budget, simply introducing a workplace innovation programme would imply a commensurate reduction in funding currently allocated to testing new approaches to skills development.

Workforce innovation centers could also play a key role in building a repository of good practice around workplace innovation. They are well-placed to do this. The NLWIC is planning to cooperate with Memorial University to build such a repository (https://mun.yaffle.ca/) of good practice in workforce development, for example. Once an evidence base of case studies is established, this knowledge should be aggregated systematically then disseminated via online platforms, diagnostic surveys, conferences and seminars. Canada could consider developing national standards of human resources management. These standards would serve as a benchmark for firms to aspire to in building effective learning organisations.

Ontario's **Local Employment Planning Councils** could also play a role in promoting skills utilisation and learning organisations within workplaces. They could support dissemination efforts by leveraging their strong employer networks and further developing existing HR learning resources (e.g. Employer Help Lines, HR toolkits, HR in a box) to disseminate best practice on HPWP.

International experience shows clearly that national leadership can give skills utilisation strategies much needed momentum. Canada does not have a national workforce development strategy (unlike Australia, another federal country). **Future Skills** could provide useful national leadership in the prioritisation of skills use and the promotion of learning organisations. A key component of successful skills utilisation strategies is the integration of economic development and skills policies (Keep, 2016[17]). The Future Skills Council includes members from various sectors and a representative from ESDC. Involving the federal department responsible for economic development (Innovation, Science and Economic Development Canada) in the Council would support the development of a skills utilisation strategy based on the integration of economic development and skills policies.

Recommendations

- Prioritise skills utilisation and the promotion of learning organisations in the provincial workforce development strategies. Workforce innovation centers and the Future Skills Centre could direct a portion of funding to test new approaches to skills utilisation within workplaces, in close collaboration with social partners. Future Skills could assume a leadership role in prioritising skills utilisation as a workforce development objective.

- Workforce innovation centers and the Future Skills Centre should build a repository of best practices in workforce development (including HPWPs). Ontario's LEPCs and other local actors could support the dissemination of good practice through HR learning resources, e.g. HR toolkits for employers. The Canadian government should develop national HR management standards that would serve as a benchmark for firms to aspire to in building effective learning organisations.

- To track progress, Canada could initiate a regular national employer survey that monitors work organisation, job design, management and training practices, as well as skills gaps.

References

Alasoini, T. (2019), *The Promotion of Workplace Innovation in Finland*, Finnish Institute of Occupational Health.   [42]

Anact (2019), *Services et outils du réseau Anact-Aract*, https://www.anact.fr/les-services-et-outils-proposes-par-le-reseau-anact-aract.   [53]

Anact (2017), *Appel à projets "Innovations organisationnelles et managériales"*, https://www.anact.fr/appel-projets-innovations-organisationnelles-et-manageriales.   [57]

Appelbaum, E. and R. Batt (1994), *The new American workplace : transforming work systems in the United States*, ILR Press.   [38]

Arnkil, R. (2004), "The Finnish workplace development programme: A small giant?", *Concepts and TransformationConcepts and Transformation International Journal of Action Research and Organizational Renewal*, Vol. 9/3, pp. 249-278, http://dx.doi.org/10.1075/cat.9.3.03arn.   [45]

Arntz, M., T. Gregory and U. Zierahn (2016), "The Risk of Automation for Jobs in OECD Countries: A Comparative Analysis", *OECD Social, Employment and Migration Working Papers*, No. 189, OECD Publishing, Paris, https://dx.doi.org/10.1787/5jlz9h56dvq7-en.   [5]

Ashton, D. and J. Sung (2002), "Supporting Workplace Learning for High Performance Working", https://www.researchgate.net/publication/44833376 (accessed on 9 August 2019).   [11]

Belt, V. and L. Giles (2009), "High performance working: a synthesis of key literature".   [26]

Bloom, N., R. Sadun and J. Reenen (2016), *Management as a Technology?*, Harvard Business School.   [21]

Business Decisions Ltd (2002), *New Forms of Work Organisation: The Obstacles to Wider Diffusion*, DG Employment and Social Affairs, Brussels: European Commission. [27]

Cappelli, P. (1996), "Technology and skill requirements: implications for establishment wage structures", *New England Economic Review* May, pp. 139-156. [10]

Cappelli, P. and N. Rogovsky (1994), "New work systems and skill requirements", *International labour review*, Vol. 133/2. [9]

Costen, W. and J. Salazar (2011), "The Impact of Training and Development on Employee Job Satisfaction, Loyalty, and Intent to Stay in the Lodging Industry", *Journal of Human Resources in Hospitality & Tourism*, Vol. 10/3, pp. 273-284, http://dx.doi.org/10.1080/15332845.2011.555734. [18]

Döös, M. and L. Wilhelmson (2009), *Organising Work for Innovation and Growth. Experiences and efforts in ten companies*, VINNOVA – Verket för Innovationssystem / Swedish Governmental Agency for Innovation Systems. [33]

Eurofound (2016), *Workplace innovation in the public sector*, https://web.archive.org/web/20160322041437/http://www.eurofound.europa.eu/news/spotlight-on-win-win-practices/workplace-innovation-in-the-public-sector. [47]

Eurofound (2015), *Third European Company Survey – Workplace innovation in European companies*, Publications Office of the European Union, Luxembourg. [59]

European Commission (2014), "Workplace Innovation: Concepts and indicators". [4]

Exton, R. and P. Totterdill (2019), "Unleashing workplace innovation in Scotland", *International Journal of Technology Transfer and Commercialisation*, Vol. 16/3, p. 228, http://dx.doi.org/10.1504/ijttc.2019.10021356. [43]

Fialho, P., G. Quintini and M. Vandeweyer (2019), "Returns to different forms of job-related training: Factoring in informal learning", *OECD Social Employment and Migration working paper, Forthcoming, OECD.*, OECD. [8]

Godard, J. and J. Delaney (2000), *Reflections on the "High Performance" Paradigm's Implications for Industrial Policy*. [24]

Granados, P. and G. Quintini (forthcoming), "External and Internal Motivation Behind Skills Deployment at Work", *OECD Publishing*. [29]

Gunderson, M. (2015), *Changing pressures affecting the workplace and implications for employment standards and labour relations legislation*, Ontario Ministry of Labour, https://cirhr.library.utoronto.ca/sites/cirhr.library.utoronto.ca/files/research-projects/Gunderson-3-Changing%20Pressures%20Trends.pdf (accessed on 9 December 2019). [28]

Harris, L. et al. (2011), *A Review of the 'Innovative Workplaces' Initiative*, http://www.acas.org.uk/researchpapers. [56]

Healy, J. (2003), *Skills for the future ministerial inquiry: high performance work practices*, Government of South Australia. [39]

HRSDC (2012), "Evaluation of the Workplace Skills Initiative", Strategic Policy and Research Branch, Human Resources and Skills Development Canada, Final Report, http://www12.hrsdc.gc.ca. [44]

Jameson, H. (2012), *Making skills work Trade unions and their role in optimising the use of skills in the workplace*, http://www.ipa-involve.com (accessed on 9 December 2019). [55]

Johnston, R. and G. Hawke (2002), *Case studies of organisations with established learning cultures*, NCVER, http://www.ncver.edu.au. [2]

Keep, E. (2016), "Improving Skills Utilisation in the UK-Some Reflections on What, Who and How?", http://www.skope.ox.ac.uk (accessed on 5 December 2019). [17]

Kennett, G. (2013), "The impact of training practices on individual, organisation, and industry skill development", *Australian Bulletin of Labour*, Vol. 39/1, pp. 112-135, https://econpapers.repec.org/scripts/redir.pf?u=http%3A%2F%2Fhdl.handle.net%2F2328%2F27684;h=repec:fli:journl:27684. [19]

LO (2007), *Employee-driven innovation – a trade union priority for growth and job creation in a globalised economy*, LO, The Danish Confederation of Trade Unions. [54]

Lowe, G. (2000), *The Quality of Work: A People-Centred Agenda*, Oxford University Press, Toronto. [25]

Lynch, L. and S. Black (1998), "Beyond the Incidence of Employer-Provided Training", *Industrial and Labor Relations Review*, Vol. 52/1, p. 64, http://dx.doi.org/10.2307/2525243. [7]

Martini, M. and D. Cavenago (2017), "The role of perceived workplace development opportunities in enhancing individual employability", *International Journal of Training and Development*, Vol. 21/1, pp. 18-34, http://dx.doi.org/10.1111/ijtd.12091. [14]

Memon, M., R. Salleh and M. Baharom (2016), "The link between training satisfaction, work engagement and turnover intention", *European Journal of Training and Development*, Vol. 40/6, pp. 407-429, http://dx.doi.org/10.1108/ejtd-10-2015-0077. [20]

NCCP (2007), *Irish Workplaces: A Strategy for Change, Innovation and Partnership 2007–10*, National Centre for Partnership and Performance, Dublin. [52]

OECD (2019), *Getting Skills Right: Future-Ready Adult Learning Systems*, Getting Skills Right, OECD Publishing, Paris, https://dx.doi.org/10.1787/9789264311756-en. [15]

OECD (2018), *Case Study: Free agents and GC talent cloud - Canada*, https://www.oecd.org/gov/innovative-government/Canada-case-study-UAE-report-2018.pdf. [50]

OECD (2017), *Fostering Innovation in the Public Sector*, OECD Publishing, Paris, https://dx.doi.org/10.1787/9789264270879-en. [48]

OECD (2016), *OECD Employment Outlook 2016*, OECD Publishing, Paris, https://doi.org/10.1787/empl_outlook-2016-en. [3]

OECD (2010), *Innovative Workplaces: Making Better Use of Skills within Organisations*, OECD Publishing, Paris, https://dx.doi.org/10.1787/9789264095687-en. [1]

OECD (forthcoming), *Preparing for the Future of Work in Canada*, OECD Reviews on Local Job Creation, OECD Publishing, Paris. [58]

OECD/ILO (2017), *Better Use of Skills in the Workplace: Why It Matters for Productivity and Local Jobs*, OECD Publishing, Paris, https://dx.doi.org/10.1787/9789264281394-en. [13]

Oeij, P., D. Rus and F. Pot (eds.) (2017), *Workplace Innovation*, Springer International Publishing, Cham, http://dx.doi.org/10.1007/978-3-319-56333-6. [40]

Oosi, O. et al. (2010), "Arjen muutoksista työelämän innovaatiotoiminnaksi – Työelämän kehittämisohjelma 2004-10 Arviointiraportti", No. No. 5/2010, Tekes Programme Report, Helsinki. [46]

Oracle (2019), "The 2019 State of Artificial Intelligence in Talent Acquisition", HR Research Institute, https://www.oracle.com/a/ocom/docs/artificial-intelligence-in-talent-acquisition.pdf. [35]

Osterman, P. (2008), "Improving Job Quality: Policies Aimed at the Demand Side of the Low-Wage labor Market", in *A Future of Good Jobs? America's Challenge in the Global Economy*, W.E. Upjohn Institute, http://dx.doi.org/10.17848/9781435641037.ch6. [22]

Osterman, P. (1995), "Skill, Training, and Work Organization in American Establishments", *Industrial Relations*, Vol. 34/2, pp. 125-146, http://dx.doi.org/10.1111/j.1468-232X.1995.tb00365.x. [6]

PSE (2013), *Creating an Innovative Public Sector*, New South Wales Government, New South Wales, https://www.psc.nsw.gov.au/ArticleDocuments/1499/IDEAS_AT_WORK-Innovation_Doc_Full.pdf.aspx. [49]

Quintini, G. (2014), "Skills at Work: How Skills and their Use Matter in the Labour Market", *OECD Social, Employment and Migration Working Papers*, No. 158, OECD Publishing, Paris, https://dx.doi.org/10.1787/5jz44fdfjm7j-en. [30]

Skills Australia (2012), *Better use of skills, better outcomes: A research report on skills utilisation in Australia*. [12]

Skills Australia (2010), *Australian Workforce Futures A National Workforce Development Strategy*, https://www.voced.edu.au/content/ngv%3A36130. [32]

Stone, I. (2011), *International approaches to high performance working*, UK Commission for Employment and Skills, London, https://www.gov.uk/government/publications/international-approaches-to-high-performance-working. [31]

Stone, I. (2011), "International approaches to high performance working. Project Report.", UK Commission for Employment and Skills, London, http://www.ukces.org.uk/publications/er37-international-approaches. [41]

Stone, I. and P. Braidford (2008), "Engaging small employers in continuing training: an international review of policies and initiatives". [51]

Stone, I. et al. (2012), *Promoting high performance working*, https://assets.publishing.service.gov.uk/government/uploads/system/uploads/attachment_data/file/34638/12-1195-promoting-high-performance-working.pdf. [34]

Totterdill, P. et al. (2009), *Workplace Innovation in European Countries*, Report to KOWIN. UK Work Organisation Network, Nottingham. [16]

Winterbotham, M. et al. (2013), *Skills Utilisation in the Construction Sector Final Report Prepared for CITB By IFF Research*.   [23]

Workplace Innovation Europe (2019a), *The Workplace Innovation Diagnostic*, http://www.workplaceinnovation.eu/LWIP-The-Workplace-Innovation-Diagnostic.   [37]

Workplace Innovation Europe (2019b), *Workplace Innovation Europe*, https://workplaceinnovation.eu/.   [36]

www.ingramcontent.com/pod-product-compliance
Lightning Source LLC
Chambersburg PA
CBHW081512200326
41518CB00015B/2475